Lacrosse for Beginners

LEARN HOW to play the fast-moving, exciting game of lacrosse. And, if you already know how to play, learn how to play even better. Here's all you need to know about this ancient Indian sport: how to handle the ball on the run, the face-off, the basics of playing both attack and defense, attack and defense strategies. Lacrosse is a thrilling, action-packed game —a great sport for every boy and girl.

Lacrosse for Beginners

STUART JAMES

Illustrations by Robert Harford

JULIAN MESSNER
NEW YORK

Manufactured in the United States of America.
Design by Irving Perkins Associates

Library of Congress Cataloging in Publication Data
James, Stuart
Lacrosse for beginners.

Bibliography: p.
Includes index.
1. Lacrosse—Juvenile literature.   I. Title.
GV989.J35   796.34'7   80–27810
ISBN 0–671–34050–6

Acknowledgments

SPECIAL THANKS to the coaches and players of the lacrosse teams of Greenwich High School, Greenwich, Connecticut, who were willing to devote their time and special knowledge to a project that they felt might bring other young people into the sport.

Chris Coyle
former All-American
Head Coach
Greenwich High Boys' Lacrosse
Mike Monick
Head Coach
Greenwich High Girls' Lacrosse

TO ALL the young people who tolerated a photographer dogging their steps to record every dropped ball and missed shot: you were great, and you were fun.

Contents

1

THE BASICS

LACROSSE IS a simple game. A team of ten players uses sticks with baskets on one end to carry or throw a small ball up or down a field approximately 100 yards long, tossing the ball into a stationary net at the far end to score a point. To make this feat more interesting, a second team of ten players similarly armed does its best to prevent the first team from getting down the field and putting the ball into the net. If the second team can get possession of the ball, the roles are reversed, and those players race down the field to try and throw the ball into a net at the opposite end, with the first team doing whatever possible to stop them.

This, essentially, is what the game is all about. The skills and strategies required to move the ball up and down the field are something else, however. It is generally agreed that an athletic person in good condition can learn the basics of lacrosse in about two weeks. It is also known that to become skilled enough to play college or club lacrosse, it takes years of dedicated practice.

Contrary to the popular misconception of the sport, brute force is neither necessary nor an asset in playing the game. When lacrosse is well played, it is about as rough as soccer or basketball. When skills are lacking and officiating is not the best, the game can be a bit brutal. This is understandable when you consider that you can have as many as twelve players battling in a cluster for possession of a loose ball, pushing, jabbing, and swinging with their sticks. For this reason the male players wear helmets and face masks, shoulder pads, thick gloves, and articulated shields for the entire arm. In the girls' game, where no contact is allowed, no protective gear is worn except by the goalie.

Speed, endurance, and manual dexterity are the things that stand out in a good lacrosse player. There are ample reasons why the game is often called, "the fastest game on two feet." It is considerably faster than soccer or hockey. Held in the basket of the stick, the ball can be carried down the field at a full sprint. It can be thrown the length of the field with more force than a baseball. There are no rest periods and few time-outs, and the game explodes up and down the field with unrelenting pressure. Since the ball cannot be touched with the hands at any time, it must be picked up, carried, thrown, and caught with the stick. Since this is usually done on the run, the stick must become an extension of the player's arms and hands.

There is no average size for a good lacrosse player. A big person can play the game, but he must have speed and agility. If he is all bulk and muscle, a smaller player will run circles around him. In this game even the goalie has to be able to cut, run, dodge, and even sprint up the field to clear a ball.

The History of the Game

Lacrosse received its modern name from the French fur trappers who came to North America early in the sixteenth century and learned the game from the Algonquin and Mohawk Indians. The Indians played a wild game. There was no limitation on the size of the teams; there were no rules, no time-outs, and the boundaries of the playing field were loosely decided on the day of the game. There could be as many as a hundred men on the field in a big game between villages. They used a hard wooden ball wrapped with leather, and each player carried a stick that was wide at one end with a spoon-like pocket carved into it. The ball was carried in the pocket and thrown in much the same manner as it is today. The Indians called the game *baggataway*, but after watching a few games played in the wild and strenuous style of the day, the French trappers called it "la crosse," their word for "the club."

A game played between two Indian villages was usually a major event, and on many occasions it became regular combat. The game culminated in a feast and dance. Tribal members would spend a week or two preparing for the game. The players would be painted for the occasion. The two chiefs would decide on the boundaries for the game and goalposts would be erected. With the teams assembled on the field, one of the chiefs would toss the ball into the air, starting the game. The object was for one of the players to run the ball through the opposition's goalposts, and the opposition was allowed to use any means to stop him. The ball could not be touched with the hands, so a loose ball with a hundred players fighting for possession could turn into a melee. Serious injuries were common, and it wasn't unusual for several players to be killed.

One of the most famous games of lacrosse was played outside Fort Michilimackinak at what is now Mackinaw City, Michigan, and it resulted in the massacre of an entire British garrison. In a gesture of friendliness toward the hated British, Chief Pontiac of the Ottawas arranged for a lacrosse game to be played for the entertainment of the fort on June 4, 1763. The game was to be played by the Sacs and Ojibwas on the clearing in front of the fort. With the tribes and players gathered on the day of the game, the soldiers in the fort opened the gates and lounged around to watch.

As the game went on, the play surged closer and closer to the gates of the fort. On one wild toss the ball rolled inside the fort, and the two teams made a mad dash for it, the soldiers cheering them on. The Indian spectators followed the players. When they reached the open gates, the spectators suddenly produced weapons and the lacrosse game was forgotten. Traders and soldiers were killed and the fort was burned to the ground.

The British were not particularly enthusiastic about the sport, but the French trappers loved it. The sport suited their temperament. The Montreal Lacrosse Club was organized prior to 1850, and they played games with the local Indians. In 1856 the Montreal Club played the first game using field boundaries.

In 1867 the National Lacrosse Association of Canada was created, and the first rules for the game were adopted. In that same year a league was formed in Scotland, introducing the game to Europe. In the following year, the Mohawk Club of Troy, New York, brought the first organized games to the United States.

The modern lacrosse game was developed by a handful of Eastern and Southern colleges, and because it never caught on as a major college spectator sport, a kind of snobbery grew up around the game. The powerful lacrosse schools were seldom identified with any other sport on a national basis: Johns Hopkins, Hobart, Ithaca, Roanoke. All were avid lacrosse schools and perennial contenders for the National Championship. On the secondary level, it was usually the Eastern prep schools that fielded lacrosse teams.

All that has changed. In 1978 there were 156 colleges playing the game under the auspices of the NCAA and dozens more planning to adopt the sport. Hundreds of high schools were fielding teams from Connecticut to California. A semiprofessional league was playing in the East with eighty-eight games scheduled. Exposure on national television provided a major boost for the sport, and the 1980 National Championship game between Johns Hopkins and the University of Virginia drew a crowd of 56,000 spectators.

RULES

All games of men's lacrosse—scholastic, collegiate, and club—are played under the rules of the National Collegiate Athletic Association (NCAA).

The official rules are published annually in the NCAA Lacrosse Guide, and because the rules are constantly undergoing changes to make the game more competitive, it is always a good idea to consult a current guide for a rules interpretation. The guides are sold at most sporting goods stores that carry lacrosse equipment. You can, however, receive a copy of the guide directly from the NCAA by writing to NCAA Publishing Department, Box 1906, Shawnee Mission, Kansas 66222.

Girls' lacrosse has its own unique rules, and there is no way that you can fully understand this game without a copy of the rules book. The sport is governed by the United States Women's Lacrosse Association, and you can contact their executive office at Box 48, Blue Bell, Pennsylvania 19422.

The Lacrosse Foundation, Inc., is a non-profit organization devoted to spreading the good word about lacrosse and operating the Lacrosse Hall of Fame which honors the all-time lacrosse greats. The Foundation is located at the Newton H. White Athletic Center, Homewood, Baltimore, Maryland 21218.

At the Hall of Fame the Lacrosse Foundation also maintains a museum and library devoted to the sport. It also publishes *Lacrosse* magazine, with five issues a year, devoted to news on teams, games, and clubs.

The Foundation staff is eager to answer any query regarding the game of lacrosse. Their telephone number is 301-235-6882. If you are considering the creation of a lacrosse league, they will gladly offer advice and show you how others have organized successful programs. They also sponsor clinics and exhibition games. They rent films for instruction. They even have a stick loan program for teams just getting started.

For information on sports camps for boys and girls that feature lacrosse, the Foundation can supply a full and current listing. Most of these camps, incidentally, are operated by college coaches and staffed by college players.

THE FIELD OF PLAY

According to NCAA rules, which are the accepted standards in this country, the lacrosse playing field is 110 yards long and can be from 53⅓ to 60 yards wide, although 60 yards is the norm. The goals are 80 yards apart, and there is a 15-yard playing area behind each goal.

A goalpost is generally made of one and one-half-inch pipe. The two vertical posts are six feet apart and the top crossbar must be six feet from the ground. The pipe base of the goal, extending to the rear, is in the shape of a triangle. Another pipe extends from the center of the top crossbar to the apex of the base triangle. A net is attached to this triangular frame. Rules for the 1980 season decreed that the side posts and crossbar be painted orange, but this isn't always followed.

A circle called "the crease" is drawn around each goal. The crease has a radius of nine feet measured from the center of the front line of the goal. With the base of the goal extending seven feet to the rear, the "point" of the base triangle is just two feet from the rear of the crease. This is an extremely important area. Only the defending players may step into the

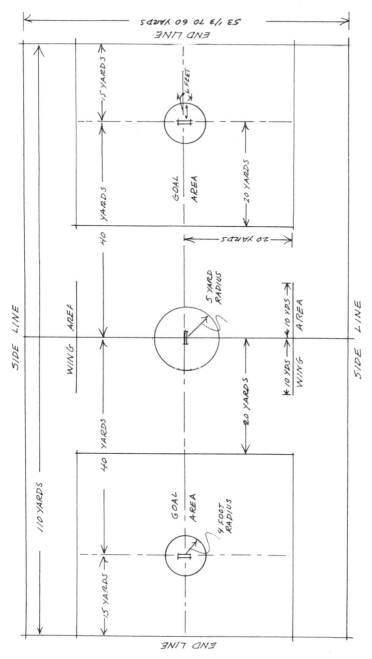

The Field of Play

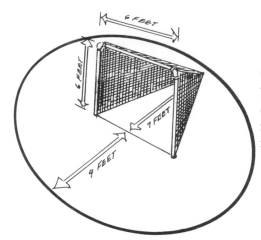

The goal is surrounded by a circle called the crease, an area where members of the attacking team may not enter.

crease area, and if an attacking player so much as extends his stick into the crease area or steps on the line, the ball is given to the defenders to play from the centerline.

The goal area is ten yards in from the sidelines and extends thirty-five yards in from the endline. It should be clearly marked.

The field is divided in half by a clearly marked centerline. This is important because, as play progresses up and down the field, the mid-field players must always be conscious of this line to make certain that they are playing on-sides. At the center of the centerline is an "X" surrounded by a plainly marked circle. This is the point where the face-offs are played.

A line twenty yards long bisects the centerline ten yards in from the sidelines to set up the wing areas. This creates two boxed areas where the mid-fielders are confined during the face-off.

Essentially, these are the official requirements for the field of play. There are also regulations governing substitution areas, coaches, areas, timer's table, and team benches. There should be two chairs on either side of the timer's table to serve as a penalty box. In most games on the scholastic level these rules are not always followed as written. There is usually a timer's table, and there might be team benches, but substitutions are often made from the centerline and penalized players sit wherever they can find space. Since the penalized player is anxious to get back into the game, he usually stays close to the timer.

THE TEAM

There are ten players on a team. Besides the goalkeeper, there are three defensemen, three mid-fielders, and three attackmen. The historical names for the positions still prevail in the rule books, although you will seldom hear them used. As the players line up on the field, they are known as: *goalkeeper, point, cover point, first defense, right wing, center, left wing, first attack, outside home, inside home.*

The goalie and the three defensemen play most of the game in the defensive half of the field. The three attackmen stay on their opponents' side. The mid-fielders, or middies, play all over the field, assisting on both defense and attack and dominating the face-off.

At all times during the game there must be at least four players of a team stationed in the defensive portion of the field. It doesn't matter who these players are. They can be defense, mid-field, or attack players as long as there are four men on the home side of the centerline. In a case where a defenseman takes the ball and runs it into the attack area, at least one of the mid-fielders must remain in the home side of the field until the defenseman returns.

Conversely, a team must always have three men in the attack side of the field. These are usually the three attackmen, but this can vary. In a case where an attackman is in hot pursuit of an opposition middie who has taken the ball, and the chase takes him over the centerline, one of his own middies

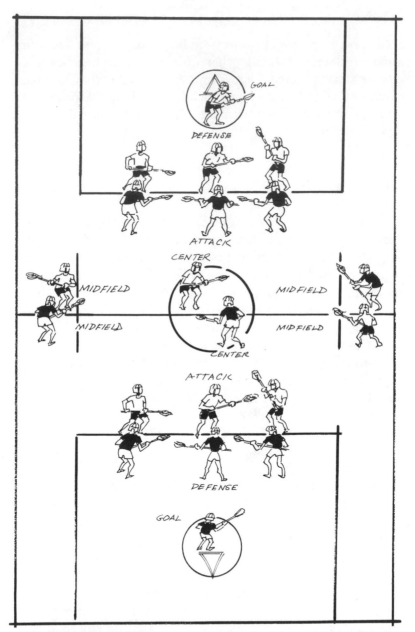

The two teams will line up somewhat in this manner at the start of a game. The attack and defense players pretty much stay in their respective sides of the field, while the midfielders range back and forth.

need only step over the centerline into the attack area to make up the required three players and keep his team on-sides.

It is legal for the goalie to run the length of the field and take a shot at the opposition goal just as long as one of the middies on his team stays in the home side of the field to maintain the complement of four players. This, however, would be a foolhardy maneuver, and there is no record of it ever having happened.

PLAYING EQUIPMENT

The ball used in lacrosse is made of solid rubber and is white or orange. It must measure between seven and three-quarter and eight inches in circumference and weigh between five and five and one-quarter ounces. When dropped from a height of seventy-two inches onto a concrete floor, it must bounce forty-three to fifty-one inches. All the lacrosse balls sold in sporting goods stores today are stamped "Meets Specs of USILA Official Rules." Check for this legend on the ball, and you'll meet the specifications.

There has been one major change in the game in recent years, and that has been in the design and construction of the stick, which is officially known as the crosse. The traditional crosse was made of hand-carved wood with a net of leather and catgut. This design is still used in the girls' game, but for the boys' game it has been changed completely. The new crosse is made of plastic, with nylon and leather for the net and aluminum for the handle.

Designed to make the game faster and ball handling more dramatic and exciting, the modern crosse, like its predecessor, has a handle and a head joined at the throat. The overall length from the end of the handle to the head must be no less than forty inches and no more than seventy-two inches, with the exception of the goalie's crosse, which can be any length. The

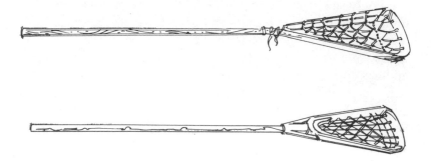

The old-style crosse is still used in the girls' game. It is fashioned of wood and gut. **The stick used in the boys' game is made of plastic and aluminum and has been redesigned to allow for greater control of the ball, making the game faster and more exciting.**

head must measure between six and one-half and ten inches, inside measurement, at the top and bottom of the wall. The wall, which is the rim of the head, cannot be more than two inches high. The measurement from the end of the head to the guard stop at the throat must be no more than ten inches. The goalie's crosse generally measures from ten to twelve inches across the inside of the head, or *face*, as it is sometimes called.

A crosse is illegal when a player has stretched the pocket in the head to the point where the ball sits below the bottom edge of the wall. This makes it difficult for an opponent to dislodge the ball and is considered unsporting.

Required protective equipment is a helmet with face mask and chin pad, and thickly padded gloves. Optional equipment includes lightweight shoulder pads of the type worn in ice hockey, and arm pads to protect the forearm, elbow, and upper arm. Soccer cleats are worn on the feet, and the uniform is generally a pair of shorts and a numbered jersey.

Besides the full array of protective equipment, the goalkeeper wears a chest protector. He also generally wears sweat-

The crosse used by the defensive player (left) has a longer shaft than the attackman's crosse shown on the right.

pants or jogging pants. The rules state that his protective gear should not exceed standard baseball equipment as far as shin guards and chest protector are concerned, but he can also wear football pants if he desires.

A fully equipped lacrosse player wears a protective helmet with face mask, fully padded gloves that cover the wrists, arm pads, shoulder pads, and a pair of cleats.

How the Game is Played

The teams take their starting positions on the field. The goalies are in the crease. The attackmen are in the goal areas, opposed by defensemen. The wingmen are in the wing areas close to the sidelines. The two centers meet at the center of the field and crouch over the centerline, facing the goal they will attack, their crosses back-to-back. This is the face-off.

When the official is ready, he places the ball between the two crosses at center field. No player may move from position until the whistle starts the game. At this signal the two centers battle for the ball and the wingmen (middies) are released from the wing areas. When one of the teams has possession of the ball, the attackmen and defensemen may move from their positions. Now the ball is moved to the goal. It can be carried, thrown, kicked, or batted along the ground with the stick, as long as it is not touched by any player's hand.

Regulation playing time is sixty minutes, but for high school games this is reduced to forty minutes, and for high school junior varsity and junior leagues it is further reduced to thirty-six minutes. In high school a game is comprised of four quarters of ten minutes each. In the younger leagues the quarters are eight minutes. There is a two-minute rest period between quarters and a ten-minute break between the halves. In some cases, where the coaches agree, there can be a fifteen-minute break between the halves.

If a game ends in a tie, there is a two-minute rest, then the teams play a three-minute (four minutes in college games) sudden death overtime, with the first team to score winning the game. If the overtime remains deadlocked, there is a rest, then another overtime until one of the teams scores.

Nineteen eighty rule changes reinstated the old system of facing-off to start each period and after every goal.

Lacrosse has a unique system for determining who gains possession of an out-of-bounds ball. If the ball goes out while being moved around the field, the offender is the last person to touch the ball and it is awarded to the other team. If the ball goes out because of a shot or deflected shot to the goal, however, the out-of-bounds ball is awarded to the player of the team trying to score who is closest to it when it goes out. The team is said to have a *free play*. After a missed shot, the players closest to the ball will make a mad dash after it to be closer than the opponents and thus gain or regain possession.

The penalty for an infraction of the rules results in the loss of the ball or expulsion from the game for a period of from thirty seconds to three minutes.

Any member of a team, including the coach, who strikes or tries to strike an opponent or an official with his hand, his crosse, or the ball will be ordered out of the game for the remainder of the playing time. If a coach gets ordered off the field, the in-home member of his attack unit must also sit out the game for a three-minute penalty period.

Any player who commits five personal fouls will be ordered out of the game, but after a three-minute penalty period a substitute can take his place.

With subtle variations, the girls' game is essentially the same as the boys'. The playing area has no measured boundaries, and the goals are 100 yards apart. The captains and officials decide on the boundaries before the start of the game, but it is left to the discretion of the officials to call a ball out of play. There are twelve girls on a team. The game runs fifty minutes in two twenty-five minute halves. In some cases substitutions are allowed only at the half, but free substitution can be the rule if the coaches agree beforehand. The girls, as we said before, still use the old-style wooden stick (crosse), and, because they use no protective gear, there are a variety of rules to insure safety in play.

Don't get the idea that the girls' game is less exciting and strenuous. It's fast. It requires great skill and finesse, and it has a tendency to get almost as rough as the boys' game.

HANDLING THE BALL

T HE HEART of the game is known as stick technique or ball handling. It is the artistry of lacrosse and the aspect that makes the game different from any other game. It looks so simple, picking up a bouncing ball with the head of the crosse while running, but it takes hours of practice.

If a boy or girl can pass, catch, and cradle the ball effectively, and do it with both hands, he or she will find a spot on most lacrosse teams.

It was not too many years ago that there were right- and left-handed lacrosse players, but not any more. With the new-style crosse, a player has to be able to go both ways to make it in today's game. It's difficult and terribly frustrating, but the novice must resign himself to long hours of conditioning his mind and body to use both hands with equal dexterity. This is equal to learning to write with the unnatural hand. Catching with either hand is not too difficult. It is a natural movement.

Right-handers, for instance, will usually catch a ball with their left hand. Learning to throw with either hand is something else, and for the first few weeks you'll be bouncing the ball off your shoelaces. But you'll get the hang of it in time. It is an absolute *must* that you be able to play with either hand if you are going to play lacrosse on the scholastic level.

How to Hold the Stick

The correct way to hold the stick is the most natural way. Standing with your arms at your sides and holding the stick horizontally, a right-hander will grip the end of the stick with his left palm down and his right hand will hold the stick, palm up, about twelve inches from the throat.

Logic dictates that a player should use as long a stick as he can handle. The longer handle gives more range for intercepting passes and reaching to check an opponent's stick and more power for throwing. In reality, however, attackmen will always go for as short a stick as possible, the legal minimum being forty inches. When you try to explain the logic of the longer stick the attackmen will tell you that the shorter stick

The correct way to hold the crosse. One hand is at the extreme end and the other is about twelve inches from the throat.

The incorrect way to hold the crosse. Both hands are too close to the throat.

Another incorrect way to hold the crosse. The right hand is in the proper position, but the left is too far down the handle.

feels better. Defensemen, on the other hand, like to be known as "the long sticks," and they will all go for the maximum allowable length.

Don't underestimate feeling right in the way you hold the stick. The ultimate in performance is when it feels like an extension of your arm and you can reach out and snag a loose ball like a webbed hand. If it feels good and it works, it's right.

Defensemen will invariably use more variation than attackmen in the way they carry the stick. Just holding the stick, you will find them using one hand a foot or two from the end of the handle. For defending against an attack, they will utilize the full length of the handle. If they intercept the ball and decide to run with it, they will generally choke up for better control of the ball. Again, experience will tell each player what feels right and what is most effective.

PASSING

The combination of the crosse and the arms makes a catapult, and when a player gets the hang of it, he can throw a ball the length of the field. The catapult effect also makes it difficult for the novice to throw accurately. The inclination is to propel the ball with wrist action, but it won't work. The throw is a combination of push and snap, but it uses both arms.

In the days of the old wooden crosse, players were taught to shovel the ball and pass from the side. In today's game there is only one correct way to pass, and that is the overhand throw. You will see all sorts of creative passing in a game invented on the spot, and hotshot collegians will do a lot of razzle-dazzle, behind-the-back passes. But the standard pass accepted by coaches everywhere is the overhand.

For a right-hander, the stick is held on the right side, the left arm crossing the body and gripping the stick at the very end. The head is tilted back over the shoulder, the ball held in

The correct stance for throwing the ball. The crosse is cocked back over the shoulder, and the left arm is extended across the chest. The left foot is extended slightly and pointed in the direction of the throw.

The actual throw is a combination pushing and flicking action. The hand on the end of the handle pulls in toward the chest and the hand closer to the throat pushes out with a snap to propel the ball.

the pocket, the right hand on about the middle of the handle. To make the throw the left hand is pulled in toward the body and the right pushes up and out.

The only way to learn how to do this well is to spend a lot of time playing catch. You can do this with another player who is also using a stick or you can just throw to a friend who catches the ball with his hands and throws it back.

Keep practicing, and once you are used to getting the ball out of the net, you can start to work on accuracy. With the stick and ball poised over the shoulder, turn slightly until the left side (if you're throwing right-handed) is in the direction you want the ball to go. Extend the left foot, which is natural in a right-handed throw of any kind, point the foot toward your target, and let the ball fly.

Passing is something that you will practice constantly for as long as you play lacrosse. There are many variations. If you have a group practicing, put them in a large circle. Get everyone to run around the circle and pass back and forth across the circle. In another exercise you can run down the field passing back and forth while on the move. In still another move, have your partner face you from across a field. You run together, and he flips the ball to you. You catch it, run past him, and then turn quickly and fire a pass to him.

Most coaches will try to get their players to stop running before they throw a pass to a teammate. This is certainly the best thing to do for accuracy, but in a game with a tight man-to-man defense, having time to stop and throw may not be possible. Learn to throw on the run.

Above all else, from the very beginning of learning to throw with the crosse, practice throwing from both sides. It is going to be awkward, and you will have a tendency to favor your natural side, but force yourself to throw both ways. Do it the correct way from the beginning, and you will save yourself a lot of frustration later.

When you reach the level where you are able to throw the

A basic exercise that is used by every lacrosse player regardless of his skill is playing catch with a teammate. The two players run down the field or in a circle, simply passing back and forth while on the move.

ball into a moving basket, you should practice the ideal throws. Try to hit a standing receiver above the outside of his shoulder at ear level. This isn't going to happen often, but it is something to try for. When throwing to a receiver running away from you, you try to put the ball over his shoulder so that he can catch it without breaking his stride. For a receiver running opposite you, determine his course and speed, and lead him and throw, trying to get the runner and ball in the same spot at the same time.

CATCHING

Catching the ball with the crosse is easier than throwing —at least for a beginner. It is a much more natural action to do with either the right or left hand. The trick in lacrosse is to be able to catch the ball in the heat of a game with an op-

A rule basic to catching is to always move in on the ball to make the catch. In these photos, the player has judged the flight of the ball and starts to run toward it, bringing his crosse up to meet the ball.

ponent swarming over you. The secret is to practice being on the move as you wait for the ball.

A receiver should never wait for the ball to reach him. This makes it easy for your opponent to intercept it. The receiver always tries to run into the ball. The face of the stick should be extended and placed in the path of the ball. As the ball hits the net, the receiver moves the stick back slightly to absorb the impact of the ball, and at the same time he gives a slight twist with the wrists. It takes some practice to do this, but it soon becomes a natural movement. Cushioning the impact of the ball as you receive the catch eliminates the possibility of it bouncing out of the net. The twisting action secures it into the pocket by centrifugal force. Don't worry about trying to understand the technicalities. In the process of catching the ball you will see that it works. The twist is always toward your face, whether caught on the right or left side. Practice the twist from both sides. The unnatural side will be more difficult, but you'll get it if you keep trying.

CATCH AND TURN

When you feel proficient at catching the ball, keeping on the move, and driving in to receive the catch, you can start making a complete turn after the catch. This is important to do in a game when your opponent is doing his best to get the ball away from you. The object of this exercise is to get the ball away from your opponent as quickly as possible. If you make the catch on the right, and your opponent is on your left, you bring the ball close to your body and pivot on your left foot, swinging your body to the right. As you shift your weight onto your right foot to complete the pivot, you also shift the stick from your right hand to your left. In this way the ball is always at the farthest point from your opponent. If he is on your right, or the catch is made on your left side, the movements are simply reversed.

The overhand catch is made by a player on the dead run. It can be thrown from behind or from the side. The catcher takes the ball over his shoulder and lets it drop into the net of the crosse. It is a move that requires a lot of practice.

THE OVERHAND CATCH

One of the more difficult catches to make is the running catch made over the shoulder, but it is extremely effective in executing a fast break, and worth practicing. The receiver holds his stick out in front and to the left or right while running downfield away from the passer, his head facing the rear. Glancing back for the pass, he decides whether he can take it at the right or left, and adjusts accordingly. As the ball comes over his shoulder, he takes it into the net, cushioning the impact, and then gives it a quick twist to secure the ball.

FOLLOWING THE BOUNCING BALL

One of the best solo exercises you can do to perfect your passing and catching skills is to find a wall you can throw the ball against and catch it. A building wall, like a warehouse, is best because you won't be constantly throwing the ball over the top of the wall. When you get good, you can run along the wall, bouncing the ball off the wall at an angle, catching

One of the best exercises a lacrosse player can indulge in is to play catch against a wall, slamming the ball and catching it on the bounce. You can do this alone, and it is the one sure way to perfect passing and catching.

and throwing. Go one way throwing right-handed, then run back throwing and catching left-handed. One former college star contends that this exercise was the single factor that changed him from a mediocre player to a NCAA Division III All-American.

CRADLING

This is a movement unique to lacrosse. The name implies the action. With the ball in the net of the crosse, the player twists the handle back and forth to move the head of the crosse like a cradle. This movement creates a centrifugal force that helps to keep the ball in the pocket.

To illustrate this, place a lacrosse ball in your hand, palm up, with the fingers just loosely cradling the ball. Move your hand around, twisting your wrist. You will notice that if you keep up the movement, you can turn your hand upside down and the ball will not fall out as long as you roll your hand back

To understand the movement of cradling the ball, take a lacrosse ball and hold it lightly in your hand. If you keep your hand moving in a rolling motion from side to side and then in an "S" form, you will find that the ball will stay in your hand without any pressure from your fingers.

up again. Almost everyone has seen the experiment where a bucket filled with water is swung in an arc over a person's head and not a drop of the water spills out. You get this same effect from cradling the ball in the net of the crosse.

Place the ball in the pocket of the net. Hold the stick across the body with the end of the handle slightly lower than the head. The hand near the throat is palm up. Tighten the fingers of this hand and curl the wrist back toward the body. Uncurl the wrist. Curl it again. Do it very slowly at first to get the movements smooth. Then you can speed it up.

The correct posture for the crosse when cradling is across the body, with the head of the stick up close to the side of the face.

Now raise the head of the stick and lower the handle until it forms a diagonal across your chest. Continue the curling and uncurling, and keep it up as you walk, turning and walking. The rhythm is important. Move the stick as vertical as possible until the ball finally falls to the ground. This will show you that it must be held at a slight angle.

When you feel that you have the movement of cradling down pat, try it on the run. Don't look at the ball. Keep the ball in the net instinctively. You will probably overdo the twisting movement at first, but after you lose the ball a few times you will naturally adjust to the desired movement.

Try this exercise. While cradling the ball in the net, bring the stick forward and down and then twist it up, just as though you were scooping water out of a barrel. You will see that the movement stops the ball from falling out of the pocket.

CATCH AND CRADLE

This movement is constantly used when playing lacrosse, so you should start to combine catching and cradling as soon as you feel skillful at both. Remember that as you catch the ball you bring the stick back and give it a twist. The twisting movement is the same as the first movement in cradling. Catch the ball, give it a twist, and begin the cradling action. Try it with a pivot, spinning away from an imaginary foe, and run down the field, cradling the ball.

SCOOPING THE BALL

This is a maneuver that arises hundreds of times in a typical lacrosse game. The player must scoop a stationary or rolling ball into the face of his crosse, lift it, cradle it, and run

Hold the crosse lightly in both hands with the ball in the net.

Twist the handle toward the body.

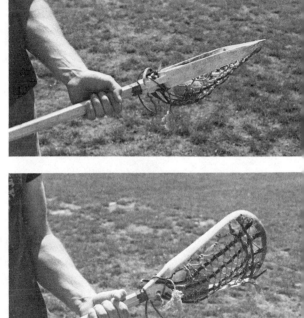

Keep turning the handle toward the body.

Turn the handle until the ball is in danger of falling from the net, then reverse the process and turn it back. Keep this up and you produce a rolling, rocking motion.

When scooping the ball, you must bend over it with the head down, bringing the leading edge of the crosse in contact with the ground just behind the ball. Keep the end of the handle close to the ground. Scoop through the ball, lifting it with a complete follow-through that will snug the ball into the pocket of the crosse. Immediately follow with the cradling movement.

or pass. More often than not, this must be done while the player is running.

This is a simple maneuver, but it must be done correctly. The player approaches the ball bent from the waist. His head is down and his knees are bent as low as possible. The right hand (if he's right-handed) is up on the throat of the stick. The tail end of the stick is low to the ground. The head touches the ground just before the ball and the ball is picked up in a smooth scooping movement, the head of the stick coming up and the tail being pushed down. Once off the ground, the ball is immediately cradled.

When a defenseman has to scoop a ground ball, he simply chokes up on his long stick, moving one hand close to the throat and sliding the other hand back until he has a comfortable stance. Once he has the ball cradled, he can move his hands back down the stick.

A word of caution to the novice: Make sure that you have the stick to one side or the other of your body when scooping the ball off the ground. If the stick should jam into the ground and the handle is pointing into your body, it could result in an injury.

A common drill for players of all levels of skill is to run up and down the field, dropping the ball ahead of them, scooping it up, and tossing it out again.

The wrong way to scoop the ball. The angle of the crosse is too sharp. To scoop effectively, the player must get down on the ball.

Scooping exercises. The players throw the balls out ahead, then run them down, scooping them up. This is repeated for the length of the field and return.

The hardest part of this maneuver is for the players to run in a crouch with the head down, and, when they reach for the ball, to keep their heads low. A good way to perfect this is to take a length of strong cord and tie it to the face mask and the handle of the stick near the throat. When the stick goes to the ground, the head has to come down with it.

A trick some coaches use to train a player to get his head down over the ball for the scoop is to tie a piece of cord from the crosse to the face mask on the helmet. In this way, the head must come down with the stick.

Another excellent exercise for developing scooping skills as they are used in a game is to have someone stand about fifty yards ahead of you, and as you run toward him, he throws the ball toward you. In this way, you judge the bounce; you pick it off the ground or out of the air. You may have to shift to the left or the right, all on the run.

TWO HANDS ON THE STICK

The beginner always finds it easier to run with the stick in one hand, but it is not a good move in lacrosse. From the very beginning, you should do every maneuver with two hands on the stick.

A stick held in one hand has a long exposed handle; a good defensemen will go after it, knowing that a tap on the end of the handle will undoubtedly dislodge the ball from the pocket.

If you go after a loose ball with the stick held in one hand, you do not have it totally under control. If you are using only one hand with a long stick, you do not have the leverage or force to fight the player for the ball. You must realize that the moment you bring the ball off the ground, cradling it into the pocket, you should be ready to make a pass to a teammate. If you are playing one-handed, you lose valuable time while you bring the other hand into play.

However, there are a couple of exceptions to the rule.

When an attackman is rolling and dodging, trying to carry the ball into scoring position near the goal, and the defenseman is going after the ball, it is advisable for the attackman to hold the crosse in one hand, extended as far away as possible from the defenseman. He can then use his free hand to ward off the probes of the defender's stick.

Another instance where it is all right to hold the crosse in one hand is when a defenseman has the ball and the attack-

An exception to the rule that two hands should always be on the crosse. The attackman extends the crosse in one hand to keep the ball as far away from the defender as possible.

man must try to stop his movement. The attackman is now at a disadvantage with his shorter stick, so it is advisable for him to hold his stick in one hand, fully extending it to inhibit his opponent's movements.

Another exception to the two-hands-on-the-stick rule. Here a defenseman has the ball. An attackman who suddenly finds himself in the defensive situation will hold the crosse in one hand so that he can extend it at arm's length to make a play for the ball or block a pass.

Checking the Stick

Striking an opponent's stick in an effort to dislodge the ball or prevent him from making a catch is called *checking*. According to NCAA rules, a player may check his opponent's crosse with his own crosse when the opponent has possession of the ball or if he is within five yards of a loose ball or a ball in flight.

If an opponent is scooping a ball off the ground, you check him by bringing your own stick sharply down on top of his. If he already has the ball, it will probably bounce out of the net and you can go after it. If he hasn't reached the ball, you have inhibited his movement, and you can then go after the ball yourself. This is called *checking down*.

Checking up is striking your opponent's crosse from beneath to knock the ball into the air.

Checking a player's crosse means bringing your own crosse down on your opponent's in an effort to stop him from scooping the ball or to dislodge the ball from the net.

An effective checking maneuver that takes great accuracy to execute is to check the handle of the stick from behind. Your opponent is crouched down, scooping the ball; you come from behind, reach out with your crosse, and tap the handle end of his stick. This will send the ball flying.

As we mentioned before, if you have an opponent carrying the ball with one hand on his stick, try to get a shot at the loose handle.

Checking is an important part of the game, and it should be done with authority. If you keep in mind that you are after the ball and not trying to inflict damage on another player, you will be able to check with force without being called for unnecessary roughness. On the other hand, if you raise your stick over your head and bring it down like an axe, an alert official will call you for it and your team will have to play a full minute with a man short.

If you swing your crosse down with force and you strike

Checking from behind, the player strikes the handle of the crosse of the player making the scoop. This will cause the ball to be knocked loose.

your opponent across the arm instead of checking his crosse, you can be called for slashing. You can get penalized for up to three minutes if the official thinks that you did it intentionally.

In checking, you won't run afoul of the officials if you focus your attention on the ball and use your stick to get it loose.

Checking an opponent's stick just before he receives a pass is effective, but tricky. Remember that the ball in flight must be within five yards of him. If you check too soon, you will be called for interference. You have to time yourself carefully. The opponent will be concentrating on making the catch. Watch him. Just before the ball reaches him, shove your stick in the face of his stick, or strike his stick out of the way.

Practice checking by having one player go out to scoop a loose ball off the ground and have another player leave the starting point two seconds later and try to check the first player's stick as he gets the ball.

This chapter has discussed the basic moves of lacrosse. Now we will relate them to the constant movement of the game.

3

THE FACE-OFF

Every lacrosse game is started with a face-off between the centers of both teams at the center of the field. There is also a face-off to open each quarter and after a goal is scored. In a situation where a ball goes out of bounds and the official has no idea who was responsible, he will call a face-off on the spot.

The official rule regarding the face-off states: "The players facing shall stand on the same side of the center line of the field as the goal each is defending, with their crosses resting on the ground along the center line."

Gripping the crosse in both hands, the players crouch down and place the crosse on the centerline. The knuckles of their gloves are resting on the ground. The faces of the two crosses are back-to-back, but they are not supposed to touch. The two centers are side-by-side and facing each other.

The official places the ball carefully between the two reversed faces of the sticks. Now they are ready to draw.

The players of both sides are frozen in position until the

Facing off, the two centers crouch over their sticks at mid-field. The crosses are back to back and the ball is placed between them. At the whistle the two players battle for possession of the ball.

draw is executed. Attackers and defensemen must stay in their goal areas. The mid-fielders are confined to the wing areas.

When the whistle is blown, the two centers struggle for possession of the ball, or at least to get it into the possession of one of their teammates. The wingmen are released from their areas so they can join in the struggle for possession. The attack and defense players cannot touch the ball until it has been in possession of one of the players on either side.

In facing on other parts of the field, the official lines up the two players so that they are "placed at right angles to an imaginary line running from the ball to the nearest goal." In this case no player can be closer than ten yards to the face-off. This type of face-off must never be held closer than twenty yards to either goal.

It takes strength, cleverness, or a combination of both to win the draw. In some cases, a player can just push through the other player's crosse. Or he might let the other player push the ball out, then quickly scoop it up when it is loose. Winning a face-off is a skill that can only come from constant practice, but it is well worth perfecting. If a team can consistently come up with the ball after a face-off, it has the advantage of an assault on the opponents' goal.

BASICS OF PLAYING ATTACK

WHENEVER A team has possession of the ball, it immediately goes on the attack.

If a defenseman intercepts a pass in his goal zone, his sole thought is to clear the ball and get it across the centerline and into the hands of the attack unit.

This attack unit consists of the three attackmen, also known as *close attack*, and the three mid-fielders. These are the players who generally score the goals.

The technical names for the attack players starting at the goal and working out to the centerline are *in-home, out-home*, and *first attack*. In actual practice you will hear them referred to as *point, crease*, and *first attack*. As an offense gets underway, the three attackmen will generally be stationed in this way: one behind the goal, one on the crease before the goal, and one just inside of the goal area, about fifteen yards from the crease.

In most cases it is the job of the mid-fielders to bring the

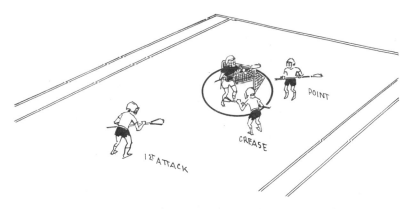

CREASE

POINT

1ST ATTACK

**The basic attack formation has one attack player at the point, a
second man in front of the crease, and the third man about
fifteen yards out from the crease.**

ball into the opposition territory to make the assault on their
goal. This is not always the case, however. If a defenseman
gets the ball and sees an opportunity to make a fast break and
take the ball down for a shot at the goal—utilizing the element
of surprise and the advantage of temporarily having an extra
man in the goal area—he will make the attack.

For the most part, it is the attack and mid-field players
who manage the scoring drives.

It would be orderly to say that the three attackmen play
point, crease, and the position fifteen yards out, and that the
middies move in and around the goal area looking for a chance
to shoot for the goal. But this is not the way it works. The three
prime positions are strategically important, but they can be
played by any of the six attack players. It is important only
that they always be covered. If one of the players moves out
of any of the three positions, another man should move into it.

Here's how these positions function in a typical offensive
play. A mid-fielder is bringing the ball over the centerline.
The three attackmen are on station at point, crease, and first
attack. The mid-fielder is alone, and he runs down the right
side of the field. The defender who has been covering the man
on point breaks away and picks up the mid-fielder, covering
him closely. The mid-fielder passes to the man on point, then

he fakes his defender off and cuts into the center. The point-man passes the ball back to the cutting mid-fielder. Meanwhile, the man on crease sees the play developing. He takes a step back and to his right, moving his defender away from the goal and providing a screen for the attacking mid-fielder. The first attackman has shifted to the right to back up the pass that he knew would be coming from the point to the cutting mid-fielder. But the mid-fielder has caught the pass, and he runs close behind his own man on crease, using him as a screen. Just as the mid-fielder passes his man, he wings his shot at the goal. The pointman is now in position to back up the shot, in the event it is missed.

In this typical play, a midfielder (1) brings the ball down the right side of the field. The man defending at point moves out and stops the middie at "2," but leaves the attackman open on the point. The middie passes to his man behind the goal, then cuts and runs to "3," taking a quick pass back from the man on the point. The attacker on the crease sees the play developing, so he steps back to make his defender follow him away from the crease. The attackman on the outside moves to the right to back up the pass in case the middie should miss it. This is the "cut and pass" play the way a coach would dream of it working. In reality, the defenders are not so easily fooled, and there is also a goalie in the picture to thwart the shot on goal.

Playing the Point

The position behind the goal is one of the strongest for the attack. The principal role for the man on point is to take passes and feed the ball to players taking shots at the goal, and then to back up shots on the goal. It was mentioned earlier that when a shot for the goal goes out of bounds, the ball is returned to the player on the offensive team nearest the ball where it goes out. It is a duty of the man playing point to make a mad dash after a missed shot going over the end line. In this way he is instrumental in keeping the ball in scoring territory.

If it sounds like this position is static, it isn't. A good pointman will stay in position when an offensive gets under-way, but that doesn't mean that he stays behind the goal all during an attack and merely passes the ball back and forth. In many cases there will be two attackers behind the goal, and the man on the point will drive out in front of the crease, a middie, or another attackman taking his place at the point.

The man on point is always a potential scorer. From his vantage point he can closely follow the movement of the ball and the positions of all the defensemen, including the goalie. He has a distinct advantage over the goalie, because while the ball is in front of the net, the goalie must have his back turned to the point. In many instances, when the goalie is playing off one side of the net, the point can move to the unprotected side, take a pass, jump up to the edge of the crease, and flip the ball into the net. He can also drive in from the point, take a pass from the sides or from the first attack position, and shoot for the goal.

Playing the Crease

The man on the crease has to be fast and an expert stick handler. One of his prime duties is to go after loose balls after they have been rebounded by the goalie and make a second try for a goal. Since this area in front of the goal is usually closely guarded, with sticks checking every move, the creaseman must be able to recover a ball and shoot in almost the same movement.

Another of the creaseman's duties is to block the goalie's view of what is going on, fake him to one side or the other, and generally get in his way.

If the pointman is out of position, possibly up front making a shot, the creaseman takes over the point, backing up shots. In this case another player moves into the crease position.

PLAYING FIRST ATTACK

This man, playing fifteen yards up the field from the crease, is a shooter. He is out of the melee in front of the goal, but he is always ready to move in to take a pass and shoot for a goal, and he should be able to make long shots on the goal. It's important to repeat that one man is not permanently assigned to this position. The players must all remain fluid while the position remains the same. When the man in the first attack position goes in to shoot for a goal or moves out of position for some other reason, another player slides in to take over the position.

DIAMOND FORMATION

One thing you will learn very quickly about lacrosse is that there are few rigid rules of play. The game is so fast and changes come so abruptly, that all plays and formations are simply suggestions that can be used to get you out of trouble if everything else fails.

A significant factor in any attack on the goal is to keep all positions covered, but it is also important to keep the attack moving fast and with precision. One way to do this is to avoid crowding around the front of the crease, keeping a wide stance on the movement of the ball. The diamond formation helps to achieve this.

With three players on point, crease, and first attack, two mid-fielders take up positions midway between crease and first attack and off to either side. The third attack player can play opposite the point, ranging from behind the goal up to the front of the crease.

Putting the ball into play from this formation gives you plenty of room to ramble. The defensemen have to spread out to cover you if they are playing man-to-man, and this gives the attackmen more opportunities to cut and dodge, set up "freelance" play situations, and make fast breaks toward the goal.

Another important factor in keeping the attack formation from jamming up at the goal is the *very important* need for

The "Diamond Formation," shown here with just the attack players in position, keeps the game open and fast-moving and eliminates crowding at the crease.

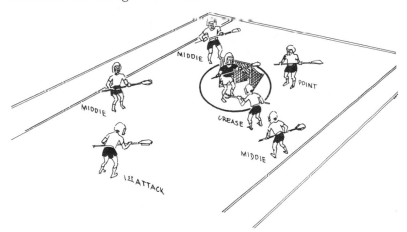

the area near the centerline to be covered in the event the opposition gets the ball and makes a break upfield.

Balance is important in the attack. At no time should all the players be bunched in one area of the field. The attack-men should always be in motion, constantly changing. The passes should be short and crisp. If an attack unit can set up fast and move the ball with authority, it produces a positive psychological advantage over the defense unit.

RUNNING BEHIND

Too many attack units believe that the only area for moving the ball is in front of the crease. This is not good strategy. It is always advantageous for an attack unit to carry the ball behind the goal. It opens up the defense and gives more range to the attack.

Imagine that an attacker comes down the right side of the field. There is no player open to take a pass. He runs behind and around the rear of the goal. The defender follows him, and the goalie has to shift, following the ball. As the attacker runs out to the right, he suddenly turns and passes back to the point. The defenseman has to stop and spin, looking back to see what the situation is. The goalie has to make a fast shift over to the other side of the goal. The middie cuts around the confused defender and angles in toward the crease. The point takes a step to the right and lobs the ball over the goal to the middie who catches it and flips it into the goal while the goalie is still turning to get into position.

BACKING UP

Many a game is lost because an aggressive defense unit takes over the ball after every missed pass or shot at the goal. The team that controls the ball and makes the most shots at

In the melee before the crease, the attackman makes a shot on goal. The goalie has advanced to intercept the ball, but just in case the goalie might miss and the ball go wide, the attackman behind the goalie is running into position to back up the shot.

the goal will win the game. On this basis it is vital that the attack unit try to back up every catch. Alert players who see where the pass is going to go should move into a position where they have a chance to catch or recover the ball if the catch is missed or if the pass goes wild.

It is amazing what can go on in an actual game of lacrosse. The same player who doesn't miss a ball in practice and who makes one-hand catches behind the back, suddenly, in the heat of a game, can develop four left feet and can't seem to catch anything. A sharp attack team takes nothing for granted. They'll try to back up every pass and every shot at the goal. Every ball you recover gives you another shot at the goal and keeps the game in your opponents' territory.

SCREENING

This is an important movement for players trying to shake their defensemen and shoot or pass without having a long stick in their face.

The rule book states: "Stationary and motionless offensive screening of an opponent is legal."

The way it works is simple. The attackman running with the ball is being closely pursued by a defender. He runs straight toward a teammate who is also being closely defended. The teammate stands rooted in position and offers himself as a screen. The man with the ball cuts close to his screening teammate. Meanwhile, the defender has to either run into the screen or alter his course and go around both the screen and his defending teammate who is covering the screen. Whatever he does, the attack player has gained steps on him and will be free to pass the ball or cut in for a shot at the goal.

In the basic screen play, the man with the ball (1) is being closely defended, so he runs toward a teammate, cutting close behind the teammate and forcing his defender to make a detour around two players.

CUTTING AND DODGING

One of the basic moves of all players on the attack is to get away from their defenders. The open man is a shooter.

Dodging and cutting are the maneuvers a player uses to break for daylight. The attack unit has the complete advantage here because they know what they are going to do, and the defensemen can only guess at what is coming.

The roll dodge is commonly used because it allows a ball carrier to reverse direction and protect the ball at all times. Let's say the attackman is running to the left, closely pursued by a defender. He wants to reverse field. He suddenly stops, pivots to the left on his right foot, shifts hands on the stick, throws his weight onto his left foot, and keeps running.

A simple stutter-step can be used to dodge a defender who is waiting for the ball carrier to approach. You simply fake to the right or left, then go in the opposite direction. The point to remember here is to only make one fake and then go. If you bounce back and forth, faking right, then left, then right, you are giving the defender too much time to react.

The face dodge is surprisingly effective, even against very experienced defenders. It is used when a ball carrier and a defender are face-to-face, the defender blocking the attacker's way to the goal. The attacker has his crosse up close to the right or left side of his face. He quickly curls the crosse, bringing it across to the opposite side of his face, then quickly back. Nine times out of ten the defender will be faked off-balance by the movement. On this cue, the attacker rolls to the right or left and is in the clear.

Breaking away from a defender so that you will be free to take a pass is called cutting. Since you are not the man with the ball, the defender is generally covering you with one eye. This means you can usually break away with a simple fake, and then cut in to where you want to go.

Simple but effective, the face dodge is a matter of quickly moving the cradled ball from one side of the face to the other and back. In many cases it will confuse the defense and allow you to cut or dodge.

It takes a lot of practice to perfect these movements, but it is worth the effort. You can practice roll dodges by running around cones placed on a field or any other obstacle where you can run up, make your fake, and roll.

SHOOTING FOR THE GOAL

A six-foot square may seem like an easy target, but you will be amazed at how many times an unprotected goal is missed by an experienced shooter. Shooting goals is like any target shooting. Perfection comes after a lot of practice.

Some teams hang a large T-shaped piece of plywood in the center of the goal to represent the goalie in position, then run their attack units through hours and hours of trying to fire balls past the "T" and into the net.

The upper corners of the goal are generally regarded as the most vulnerable areas. If the goalie favors his right or left side, he will be most vulnerable high on his unguarded side. A hard bouncing shot right on the crease is difficult for the goalie to play. His instinct is to go down for it; then it bounces over his head.

Inexperienced players have trouble with the long shot, seeming to feel secure only with shots off the crease. The long shot can be extremely effective, particularly if there is a lot of confusion around the crease. The shooter can fire it from the outside and close to the ground.

Most important to any attack unit is to shoot as much as possible. Shoot from inside and outside and from every angle around the goal. Only shooting produces goals. All the fancy running and passing in the world is useless if it does not produce shots on the goal.

TALK IT UP

In the confusion of an attack, it is virtually impossible for a player to know all that is going on and to pinpoint the location of all his teammates and what their intentions might be. For this reason, it is important that the players get in the habit of talking (actually, shouting) to one another when play is in progress.

"Here's your help!" an undefended mid-fielder will shout to an attackman under pressure and looking for somewhere to pass the ball.

"Watch out behind!" a player will shout to a teammate when an unseen defender is racing in to check from the rear.

"Slide over!" a player will shout to a teammate as he moves out of the first attack position and wants the position to be covered.

"Run it in!" "Take it behind!" "Pass it back!" "I'm your help!" All of these statements made in a play can be a help to a player and weld a team together.

"Regular Red Six-A!" the man running with the ball will shout when he sees that the defensive set-up is perfect for the execution of a play that the team has planned and practiced. The call is picked up by the other players; each knows his role in the play, where he is expected to go, and where the others will be going. This kind of command of a situation can have a devastating effect on a defensive unit that is even slightly unsure of itself.

A wise coach will get his players talking in every practice session and will constantly encourage a verbal exchange between the players on just about every move. In this way, talking becomes second nature and will be carried over into the game.

BASICS OF PLAYING DEFENSE

THE PRIMARY objective of a defensive unit is to stop the opposition from scoring goals. The secondary objective is to get the ball away from the opposing team on the attack and move it as quickly as possible into enemy territory for an assault on their goal. The two objectives have a tendency to blend together.

A defensive unit is composed of three defensemen, also known as *close defense*, goalkeeper, and three mid-fielders. The technical names for the three defense positions, from the goal out to centerline are: *point, cover point,* and *first defense*. In regular usage you will hear them referred to as point, crease, and first defense, and more commonly as just "D's." Some college coaches refer to their close defense as "the long sticks," in reference to the length (seventy-two inches) of their crosses.

Where a defenseman plays on the field depends in large part on the position taken by the attack player he is covering, particularly in the more common man-to-man defense.

There is real tension and excitement in playing defense. The close defense are like knights protecting a citadel. They wait in position while their teammates attack on the opposite side of the field, then suddenly there is a flurry of movement and the opposition comes charging and passing over the centerline. Now the defenders must thwart the assault, throw a screen around their goal that cannot be penetrated, and get the ball away from the opposition.

SETTING THE TEMPO

Early in the game, preferably the first time that attackmen come into the goal area, a strong defense unit will make it plain to the attackers that they do not plan to give an inch, that every pass at the goal is going to be hard-earned.

The defense has an advantage in the use of the bodycheck, and they should use it immediately. The official rules say: "Bodychecking of an opponent in possession of the ball, or within five yards of a loose ball, from the front or side above the knees and below the neck, is legal."

The body check is performed by hitting an opponent with your shoulder in the front or on the side. The player being checked must be in possession of the ball or be within five yards of a loose ball.

The bodycheck is performed by lowering your shoulder and slamming into an opponent with the shoulder. You must hit him in the front or on the side.

This move is a legal part of the game because the defense needs certain moves to overcome the natural advantages of being on the attack. The attackers know in advance what they are going to do. They have possession of the ball, and all they have to do is jockey it into position and fire it at the goal. It is impossible for a goalie to stop all shots at the goal. This isn't like soccer where the ball is large and must be kicked. The lacrosse ball is smaller than a baseball and it is flung at blinding speed. Therefore, the defensemen need some tactics to help fend off the attackers. The purpose of the bodycheck is to knock the ball carrier to the ground and dislodge the ball.

In the earliest stages of a game, the defensemen should move in on the attackers and bodycheck with authority. This does not mean that you want to hurt the other player, nor does it mean that you are going to sacrifice skills for brute force. As one coach explained it to his players, "Give 'em one good pop right off and they'll respect you for the rest of the game."

Remember that this is a legal move, a part of the game. You should practice it and you should use it.

Running Backwards and Sideways

The defenseman must stay between his man and the goal and cover every movement. He must be ready for a dodge or a cut. He should be facing his man as much as possible, and this requires some fancy footwork.

A good defenseman has to be able to run forwards, backwards, and sideways with equal speed, changing from one to the other in a split second. To practice this you should run up and down the length of the field, sprinting forward, switching to running sideways at the same speed, then backwards—always keeping up the pace. This will seem awkward at first, but it's surprisingly easy to master.

When you run sideways, you have to make sure that one foot is kept out ahead of the other at all times. In this way, you won't cross feet and get tripped up.

STAYING WITH YOUR MAN

The main function of the defenseman is to play the man, to stay between him and the goal and to keep him out of scoring range. This is not always easy to do.

A good practice exercise for all close defense is to play the attackers without sticks. Using only the gloved hands, the defender is at a marked disadvantage and must work twice as hard to keep the attackers away from the goal. When he cannot depend on his long stick for help, the defender learns to stay with his man using only his body to keep him from the goal.

When the stick is returned to the defenseman, it becomes an aid to his play instead of a crutch that takes the place of effective coverage.

A coach will often advise his defensive player to "play the numbers." This means the defender should keep his eyes on the numbers on his man's jersey, which in effect will keep the man away from the goal. The defensive player has to think of himself as being attached to a cord that is attached to the goal. As he moves around the field, playing his man, there should always be a direct line from him to the goal.

HARASSING THE ATTACK

The job of the attackers is to elude the defensemen and carry or pass the ball into the scoring territory around the front of the crease. Every move that the attackers make is

Practicing without a stick, the defenseman must work doubly hard to stay between the attacker and the goal. In this case, the attacker has managed to break away and is running in for a shot.

Defending without a stick is a popular practice ploy of many coaches. Here the defenseman is perfectly positioned to keep his man from shooting.

toward this end. It is the job of the defensemen to see that the attackers are unsuccessful.

The moment an attacker has the ball in his crosse, he is a potential threat. The defenseman playing the man with the ball must tie him up completely, but he must make every move with care. He must play the attacker close, but not so close that the man can dodge or cut around him. On the other hand, the defenseman cannot play so loose as to make it easy for the man to pass the ball.

Playing the man with the ball calls for careful aggression. The defenseman uses his long stick to advantage, jabbing at the head of his opponent's crosse, tapping the handle. He is in constant movement, but always aware that the attack player is looking for an opening to break away. He plays in a crouch, balanced on the balls of his feet. He can leap in close and make a pass at the ball, then bounce back a stick-length away from his man. He comes in again, taunts the attacker, shoves him with a gloved hand to the shoulder, then bounces back. He keeps forcing the attacker out to the sidelines. When the attacker tries to run, the long stick is in his way. When he tries to pass, the face of the long stick is in the air. When the attacker tries to fake a roll dodge, the defender is a stick-length away, waiting to pick him up and block him.

Always remember that lacrosse is a body-contact sport. A lot of players forget this. When a man with the ball starts to cut on you, lean into him, push him off. You'll break his stride, the surprise will be lost, and he'll have to run to the outside to recover, which is exactly what you want.

Use the full length of the defenseman's stick. You can stand back and still harass your man with it. If he is looking for an open man to take a pass, hold the stick in front of his face to obscure his view. When he tries to pass, give him room to get started, then meet the face of his crosse with yours.

A smart defenseman will sometimes play his man loosely, giving the impression that he has been beaten. This makes

The defenseman must harass the attacker, making it difficult or impossible for him to move the ball into the goal. In this sequence, former All-American Chris Coyle shows how it is done. His stance is low and his knees are bent; he is challenging the attacker, but is ready to counter a dodge or cut. He forces his man away from the goal, keeping the stick out ahead of the man's movement. He moves in as the man tries to cut and shoves him off with his elbow. When the attacker pivots and tries to reverse field, the long stick is out there to stop him.

Contact is important in lacrosse. When an attacker attempts to cut, the defender moves in on him, pushing with his hands and shoving him off stride.

The defenseman must learn to use his long stick to advantage. When his man is attempting to pass, he can stand back and just hold the stick in front of the opponent's face, making it difficult for him.

the man pass the ball and gives the defenseman a good chance for an interception.

DON'T GET TRAPPED

The defensive players know that the attackers will be doing everything possible to get within scoring range. The way to do this effectively is to fake the defenseman out of the play. Knowing that this is what is in the attacker's mind, the defenseman should be able to adjust accordingly.

Imagine that an attackman catches a pass and is running to the right-hand corner. A defenseman is speedily pursuing him. A smart attacker will keep running, letting the defense come right up on him, and then he will suddenly spin and reverse field. The unwary defenseman will go at least two or

A good defenseman will stay a stick-length away from his opponent when an attack play is developing. With his longer stick he can harass the attacker, but with the distance he is totally in control of the situation and cannot be beaten by his man.

three steps before he can stop and turn. By this time it is too late. The moment the man has made the catch, the smart defenseman will slow his pursuit. He knows that the man must now bring the ball into scoring range, and he, the defenseman, should be there to stop him.

A common attack move is to pass the ball, hesitate a moment to let the defenseman relax, and then cut around him and run in toward the crease, taking a return pass and trying for the score. This shouldn't happen. Look at it from the defenseman's point of view. His man has the ball and he is playing him close. The attacker throws the ball. The moment this happens, the defenseman should run backwards toward the crease, getting at least a stick-length away from his man. Now it is impossible for the man to cut toward the goal without the defenseman having him completely covered.

The single important thing for every defensive player to remember is that he cannot relax for even a split second while the ball is in his territory.

FOILING THE SCREEN

When an attack player on the move uses a teammate to screen out a pursuing defenseman, the player defending against the screen simply drops his man, shouts, "I've got him!" and takes up the man with the ball, letting the other defenseman take over his man.

It is important that there be verbal contact between the defense players.

CHECKING STICKS

The rules state that a player can check another player's stick when he is within fifteen feet (five yards) of a loose ball or a ball in the air. As soon as a ball is passed, the goalie should shout, "Check!" and every defensive player should be ready to check the stick of his opponent. Even with your back to the passer, when you are aware that the ball is in the air, you can tell from your opponent's movements and expression whether or not he is a potential receiver. In most cases, the defensive player is watching his man *and* the ball, so he knows where the pass is going.

By the time you check your opponent's crosse with your own, making it impossible for him to make a catch, the thrown ball will be within the legal distance.

If the player is on the run when the ball is passed to him, and it is difficult to check his stick, take him out of the play with a bodycheck.

PLAYING THE LOOSE BALL

It doesn't mean a thing if you make your opponent throw wild and miss catches if he recovers the ball and makes another play. The alert defenseman makes a point of battling for the loose ball.

When an attackman is scrambling for a loose ball, the defenseman should double up on him whenever possible. One defenseman shouts, "I've got ball!" and this is the signal for the second man to forget the ball and concentrate on taking the attack player out of the action. Remember that when a man is within five yards of a loose ball, the bodycheck is legal. Do it legally, being careful not to foul him from behind, but get your shoulder into him and take the man out of the play. Then your teammate can pick up the ball.

In the event of a number of players scrambling for a loose ball, a defensive player should put his head down and charge into the middle of them, concentrating totally on the ball. If you can't get your stick on it, kick it out of the crowd with your foot.

This brings up another defensive maneuver. Anytime there is a group battling for a loose ball—scuffling with sticks and kicking with their feet, checking and counterchecking, pushing and shoving—the ball will eventually make it to the outside of the crowd. In this case, it is wise for one or two defensive players to forget their man for the moment and move in close to the melee to be on hand to scoop the ball when it comes out. Even if you don't get it, you can always get back to your man.

Playing the Danger Zone

If you draw an imaginary circle from the goal out near the edge of the goal area sidelines and up to about where the first attack plays, you have sketched in the area that is most susceptible to attack. The defensive players must keep this area in their minds when they are playing man-to-man, because it is a determining factor in how they will play.

The danger zone for the defense is that area before the goal where the attackers are close enough to fire shots at the goal.

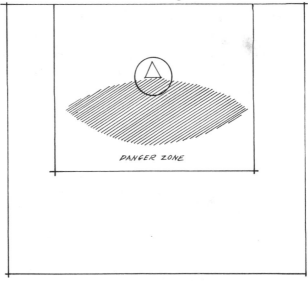

DANGER ZONE

Playing the danger zone. Attackman (4) has the ball in the corner behind the goal so his defender (4) plays him loosely, staying up near the crease. Defender (3) also plays his man loose, but wary, since his man is beyond the danger zone. Defender (1) plays his man close, but not too tight. The others are all pressing their men, ready to check a pass from (4).

Let's say that an attack player carries the ball behind the goal over to one corner. The defenseman covering this man will usually not follow him into the corner, but will station himself at the crease. The man in the corner is not a scoring threat. He either has to bring the ball up to the "danger zone" or he has to pass it. By staying on the crease and covering his man from a distance, the defensive player can pick up his man at any time, but he is also in position to lend a hand at the goal if another player should catch a pass from the man in the corner and attempt to score.

The way this zone comes into play in front of the goal depends on how the defenders play their men. If an attacking mid-fielder is playing out close to the centerline, his defender will play him at a distance, keeping a close eye on him, but staying in near the first attack position to lend a hand if he is needed closer to the goal. When the man moves in toward the danger zone, the defender plays him closer and with more intensity.

In this way, the defensemen keep as many players as possible in the vulnerable area and can more effectively hold the attackers at bay.

THE CREASE AND THE POINT

The defenseman is fully aware that both the man on the crease and on the point are dangerous. The defender covering the man on the crease knows that the attacker's job is to obstruct the goalie's view of the play, so he will do whatever is legal to clear the crease area, while he also defends against shots at the goal.

Defending against the man on point is crucial. It is an excellent spot for a good defender to intercept passes, but he must also be ready to check sticks and bodycheck when he can. But this is also a tough spot, and if the defender overplays the point, this man is always in a position to swing around the crease and score.

TALKING IT UP

Just as the attackers must talk their way through their plays, it is important for the defensemen to inform one another of everything that is going on. The leader of the defensive talk is usually the goalkeeper, but the other players must also be ready to shout out whatever they see developing.

"Take 21!" a player shouts when an attack player of that number has managed to dodge around him and is on his way into scoring territory. "I got him!" shouts a defensive teammate, as he picks up the man.

"Slide, slide!" shouts a defensive man, meaning that he is taking up the defense of a player moving into his area and that he wants another player to pick up his man.

Talking is an important part of the defense. The players would be playing alone without it, and their effectiveness would be cut in half.

6

ILLEGAL TACTICS

A PERSONAL FOUL will get a player expelled from the game for a period of from one to three minutes. More than that, it can result in a seriously injured player.

It is generally assumed that most personal fouls are committed accidentally. If it is obvious to an official that a player has deliberately committed a personal foul, the player will be ordered out of the game. After a three-minute penalty period, a substitute will take his place.

One serious foul is slashing. If you swing at an opponent's stick with "deliberate viciousness or reckless abandon," it is considered slashing, even if you don't hit the opponent's stick or body. For the most part, however, slashing is using the crosse like a club to strike an opponent. Striking any part of the face or neck of an opponent with your crosse is definitely slashing, unless you happen to be passing the ball or shooting for a goal.

Slashing is one of the most common fouls. In its most extreme form, a player slashes an opponent across the body with his crosse.

Slashing a player across the arms is also common and is a serious foul that results in ejection from the game for a time period.

It is also a slashing foul when the stick strikes any part of an opponent's head.

Bodychecking below the knees is a serious infraction of the rules and can result in injury.

Bodychecking an opponent below the knees or above the neck is another illegal move that is dangerous and should always be discouraged. Blocking with the head is known as spearing. It is illegal and dangerous. A bodycheck from behind is illegal, and if you purposely bodycheck a player after he has thrown the ball, it too is illegal.

Use of the elbow to strike an opponent in the area of the throat is a personal foul.

Crosschecking, using the handle of the crosse to strike or push an opponent, is a personal foul.

Crosse-checking is the act of slamming into an opponent with the handle of the crosse held outstretched in both hands. This is another move that can result in injury to the player being hit. It is a crosse-check if the player runs into an opponent with his crosse outstretched, or if he pushes the crosse out to strike him. Either act will result in a penalty and, in some cases, expulsion from the game.

Tripping another player with your stick or any part of your body is illegal. According to the rule book, tripping is defined as "obstructing an opponent below the knees with the crosse, hands, arms, feet or legs—by any positive primary action if the obstructing player is on his feet or by a positive secondary action if the obstructing player is not on his feet."

The tripping has to be deliberate in order to be called a foul. If you legally check a player's stick and he trips over his own stick, there is no penalty. Similarly, if you are battling an opponent for a loose ball, and while you are trying to scoop the ball up the opponent trips over your crosse, there is no penalty.

Unnecessary roughness is usually called when excessive violence is used by one player against another in what otherwise might be called a minor foul. This could be pushing or

Tripping an opponent is illegal, whether you use the crosse, as in this case, or your feet.

holding, for example, but done in an extremely violent manner.

When a bodycheck is made with unusual violence, even though it conforms to the rules otherwise, it can be called unnecessary roughness.

If a defensive player makes "deliberate and excessively violent contact" against an attack player who has set himself up as a screen for a teammate, it is a personal foul.

Fouls of a more minor nature are pushing, holding, and charging. These are simply the excesses of a body-contact sport and should be expected. That's why the players wear protective gear.

The offenses mentioned above do not belong in the game of lacrosse. It is the responsibility of the coach to teach his players the limits of body contact and to eliminate those players who insist on being violent.

When a serious injury results from illegal play, it not only hurts the individual involved, but casts a bad light on the game of lacrosse and inhibits the acceptance and popularity of the game.

7

ATTACK STRATEGY

T HE MOST valuable strategy for beginners in lacrosse is to always keep the attack simple. Complicated maneuvers like double and triple screens may be acccptable for experienced players on the college level, but for the novice the best advice is to concentrate on the basic skills to carry the game.

Strategy for the beginner should consist of maneuvers and formations that blend the basic moves into a cohesive team effort.

An attack unit that runs the ball toward the goal without any idea of what they are going to do when the defensemen close in on them is a mob with a purpose but no direction. The attack must have some basic plans. Although they'll be rather loose plans—the individual nature of the game requires that—you'll need them.

Let's look at the basic attack set-up. There's the man on the point, another on the crease, and another on first attack,

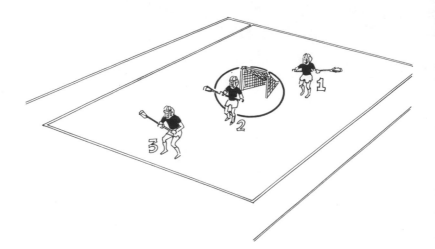

The basic attack set-up while waiting for the ball to be brought down the field is shown at the top, with a man on point, another on crease, and one outside. A slight variation on this set-up is the one up-two down formation shown in the drawing below. It brings both the point and crease players in front of the net and to the sides, allowing all three to participate in a fast-break attack play.

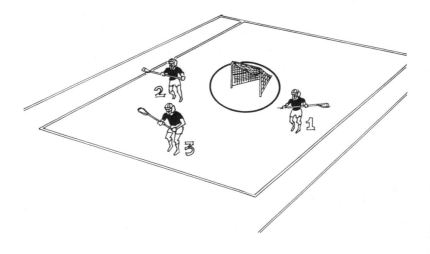

about fifteen yards out from the crease. Now let's assume that these three attackmen are waiting for their defensive unit to get the ball and bring it down to them.

In the basic set-up outlined above, the pointman is out of play. He's not going to be any help if his defensemen suddenly get the ball and want to clear it down field. So let's move the pointman up and off to the side of the crease. Take the creaseman and move him out to the other side. Now there is one man up near the centerline and two men back near the goal.

This is a logical set-up for the three attack players to position themselves while they are waiting for the ball. If they are being closely played by their defensive opponents, the two men playing back (point and crease) should play a good distance in from the sidelines. This gives them room to break away from their defenders and run out toward the sidelines if the middies bringing the ball down are having problems. They are now in good positions to take a pass.

Once the ball is safely into the goal area, the pointman runs down to take his position behind the goal, and the creaseman takes his position on the crease.

Let's say that the three attackmen are in the one up, two back formation, and the ball is passed to the crease player who is now on the right side of the field. A defensive player moves in and ties him up.

The most important thing right now is to assist the man with the ball. It is obvious that there is no chance for him to take the ball in for a shot. The mid-fielders are not yet down the field to take part in the attack. The man at first attack position is not being closely guarded, so it is easiest for him to move over and take a pass from the creaseman. The pointman, in the meantime, sees that the creaseman is busy and that the first attack is moving over to help. He slides over and covers the crease. The ball is passed back to the first attack.

The plan that has been in effect here is simple but effec-

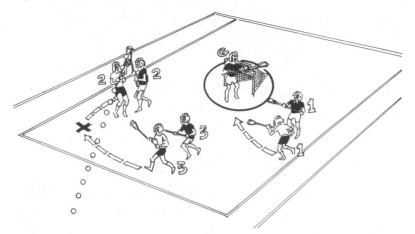

Starting with the one up-two down formation, this is how a typical attack can develop. The attack player (2) who is the crease player, but is now playing off to the side, takes a pass from down field. He is quickly covered by defender (2), so he cannot move the ball in. Attacker (3) runs over to help and takes a pass at "X." Attackman (1), who would normally be at point, goes in to cover the crease. The play has stalled. The attackers wait for their three midfielders to cross the centerline and get into the play.

tive lacrosse. The important thing in the attack is to possess the ball. The three men have accomplished that. While it is important for them to be in attacking positions, it is more important at the moment to play the ball, which they do.

Now the three mid-fielders are over the line and into the attack. One of the middies runs down the field and takes up the position at the point. The other two come on slowly, and one of them takes a pass from first attack, then passes to the other who is moving down the right side.

With the point covered by a middie, the close attack player who normally covers the position moves behind the goal on the opposite side. The creaseman moves back into the crease position. The middies and first attack, who are ranging around the outer perimeter, have control of the ball, passing it back and forth.

The object now is to get the ball into scoring range, and they have a variety of options.

It should be noted here that at every moment in an attack on the goal, it is the man with the ball who determines what the next move will be. As the man with the ball changes, so does the plan of the attackers. Everything hinges on the situation that the ball carrier finds himself in. The next move is up to him, but every other player must be constantly on the move, opening up the possibilities for bringing the ball in for a shot at the goal.

The full attack unit is now over the line. They are shown without their defenders. Attackman (3) had the ball when the middies crossed the line. He passed to middie (4), who in turn passed to another middie (5), moving the ball around to gain time and let a play develop. Attacker (2) moves back to his position at the crease and attacker (1) drops back behind the goal. The remaining middie (6) continues down the field and takes up a position behind the goal. Attackers (2, 3, 4, and 5) have set up the Diamond Formation.

Cut, Pass, and Dodge

These three moves form the basis for almost all the attack strategy once the ball is in the goal area. All the attack players other than the ball carrier should be trying to help out in the execution of one or more of them.

Let's say that the mid-fielder on the right side has the ball and is tied up by his defensive opposition. The man on the point moves out to help and takes a pass. Now the mid-fielder makes a fast cut and runs in toward the crease. The man with the ball, alert to what the middie is doing, is ready to pass the ball back to him. But he sees that the man's de-

The attack goes into action as the middie with the ball (5) passes into the corner to (6) and cuts for the crease. The receiver (6) sees that (5) is closely covered, so he passes across to his teammate (1).

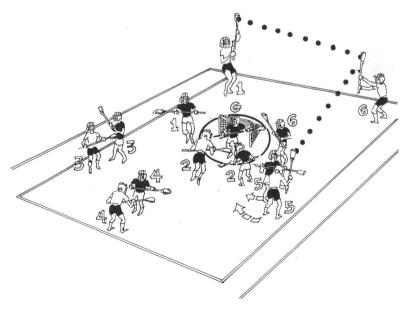

The play has shifted suddenly to the opposite side of the field and the players react. Attacker (1) has the ball behind the goal. Defender (3) moves in to cover his man, but he comes too close, and his man (3) is able to break away and cut for the middle. The point man (1) sees the break and passes the ball. It is caught at "X." The attacker (3) runs behind his teammate (2), using him for a screen, and takes a shot on goal. The passer (1) moves over to back up the shot.

fender is making a good play. A pass could be easily intercepted, so he doesn't make the play. Instead, he passes over to the close attack player on the far side of the field, behind the goal. This is a safe move that keeps the ball in motion.

The next move is up to the attack player in the corner with the ball and the rest of the team must play to him. He can run with the ball or he can pass it. If he runs he must get past his defenseman who is waiting by the crease for him to make his move. He can pass back to the pointman who is clear, and it looks like the middie up the left side of the field is open for a pass. If he passes to the middie, he can cut into the center, take a pass back, and try for the score. Before he can make the pass, the middie's defender takes a step over and covers his man closer. Too close. The middie is able to fake the man off, and he breaks away and cuts for the crease. The man with the ball sees the move. In another second the middie is in the clear, and the man behind the goal fires the ball. The moment he makes the pass, the man behind the goal moves over to back up the possible shot on the goal.

These are the options that are available on just about every play. Run and dodge your opponent and try for the score. Pass and then cut, and take a pass. A man without the ball makes the cut and takes a pass. There are hundreds of variations on the play we have described, but they all require pretty much the same decisions and the same basic cooperation from the players without the ball.

There are just a few basic rules. Everyone plays off the man with the ball. The attack players keep on the move, even when they don't have the ball. Never bunch up in one area of the field. Always try to have at least one man behind the goal.

This is all that a novice player has to know in terms of strategy to mount a successful attack. Keep it simple. Keep the assignments basic and easy to learn.

Slow-down Plays

There are occasions, particularly where novice players are involved, where it is important to slow down the attack and move the ball around the outside of the defense. When the excitement of the game has taken over the judgment of the players, it is important to calm things down, let everyone get his bearings, and then make some moves toward the goal.

Another occasion is when a team's defensive unit has been through a particularly grueling attack on their goal. When the ball is finally recovered and sent down the field, the attack unit gives the defensemen a few minutes R&R (rest and re-covery) by taking the ball in slowly and carefully, passing it around behind the goal and running back to the centerline before making any real moves at the goal.

An experienced team will know when to slow things down, but with beginners there should be a prearranged signal for the slow-down and it should be called from the sidelines by the coach. It can be a number or a name. "Twenty-three A!" shouts the coach, and the call is passed from player to player. As the ball whips around their perimeter, the unsuspecting defensemen will believe that they are about to be assaulted by some secret play.

RIDING THE DEFENSE

When the opposition gets the ball away from the attack unit, they have to *clear* the ball, which means getting it out of their goal area and down the field to their attack unit. When the close attack tries to stop the defense from clearing the ball, it is called *riding*.

Because the defense unit has an extra man in the goal keeper, they can usually clear without too much difficulty. But there are many times when a hard ride takes the defense-men by surprise and confuses them, and they will make a wild pass and lose the ball.

It is generally the goalie who clears the ball, taking it behind the goal until a man is clear, then passing it up the field. The close attack can put pressure on, and they should.

Calling for a *standard ride*, a close attack player will go behind the goal and put pressure on the goalie, making it im-possible for him to pass up the field. This will bring one or two defense players back to help the goalie. When he passes to another man behind the goal, other close attack players pick up this man, forcing him to pass. The more passes the defense is forced to make to bring the ball up to the centerline, the more chances they will have to lose the ball.

It is not good strategy to ride every time the defense clears the ball. Make it a surprise. On many occasions the goalie will have the ball and shout "Clear!" and the middies will bolt down the field to cross the centerline and take the attack to the opposition. This is a good time to suddenly put on the pressure, and use two men to ride the man with the ball.

PLAYING WITH AN EXTRA MAN

When the defense unit has a man out of the game for a penalty infraction, the attackers have at least half a minute to assault the goal with an extra man. In this situation it is imperative for the attacker with the ball not to let the time dwindle away with passing and running, but to move with speed, passing or running, into the crease area and fire at the goal.

It is immediately important for the attackers to know which player is not covered by a defenseman and use him in the attack. In most cases the defense will drop the man farthest from the crease, covering everyone close in. You can use this man on a pass, cut, and pass play. The man with the ball passes to the uncovered man, cuts, and runs toward the centerline. The uncovered attacker passes back to the man cutting for the centerline, then makes a charge for the crease. The pass goes back, and there is a shot at the goal.

The play can be simple, but it must come fast if the attack unit is going to cash in on its advantage.

ATTACKING AGAINST A ZONE

Don't let a zone defense throw you. It takes a really good defensive unit to use the zone effectively, and for the novice player it can be the easiest to attack against. The zone means that the defenders each protect an area around the goal instead of an individual player.

The zone players do not come out to meet the attackers, so you have all the time in the world to move around and behind the goal, making short, fast passes, and waiting for just the right moment to make your assault.

Unless the players are very experienced, most zone defenses have a tendency to bunch up around the crease, particularly when the ball is moved in. A smart attack in this case is for an attacker to run the ball in to the crease, bringing the defensive players in, then pass to the outside and let the receiver of the pass fire a low ground shot at the goal.

DEFENSE STRATEGY

PLAYING THE man and the ball is the primary strategy for the defense unit. On the secondary level there are strategic moves, positions, and formations that make the primary objective easier to realize.

As stated before, the purpose of the attack unit is to score goals; the purpose of the defense unit is to prohibit the score.

While confined to their goal area, waiting while their attack unit moves on the opponents' goal, the close defense is assigned to cover the three close attack players wherever they are playing. An exception to this is when all three attack players have stationed themselves near the centerline. In this case two defensemen would play near the centerline and the third would stay in front of the crease, near the goal.

This is a first rule of defense strategy. There must always be at least one defenseman playing near the front of the crease to assist the goalie in the event of a surprise attack.

Another strategic move pertains to how a man is played in relation to the position of the ball on the field. It is best explained if you will think of the ball as a magnet and the defense players as metal objects. As the ball moves around the goal area, the defense players are attracted toward it. The defender playing the ball carrier is virtually glued to his man. The defenders playing attackmen close to the ball maintain a close vigilance on their man, but keep close tabs on the ball. On the opposite side of the field the defenders play their men loosely, playing toward the ball. As the ball shifts, so does the posture of the defense. It is a subtle aspect, but it gives a flow of movement to the defense that involves every man with the play that the attack unit is attempting to put together.

CUT, PASS, AND DODGE

Just as the attackmen are always trying to use the pass, cut, and pass to get past the defensemen and into the crease area, the defensemen must always be on the lookout for these moves and either foil them or capitalize on them to intercept the ball.

Let's take the same play used to illustrate the moves the attack unit should make in the last chapter, but this time examine it from the defense unit's point of view.

The attackers have brought the ball over the centerline and a mid-fielder has possession on the right side of the field. A defender has him completely tied up and he can't move the ball, so he passes to the pointman behind the goal. The defense-man is aware that the best move his man can make is to cut for the center and take a pass from behind the goal. The defenseman steps back, concentrating totally on his man, but keeping a stick-length away. The middie makes the break for the center, but the defender moves with him, staying between

Using the same attack strategy as in the previous chapter, we will now show how the play can develop from the defense point of view. As before, the middie (5) has the ball, and he passes to the man behind the goal (6), then cuts for the crease.

The defender (5) expects the play and he moves with his man, staying between him and the goal, ready to check a pass. The attacker behind the goal (6) sees no chance for a play, so he passes across to the point man (1).

The attackman behind the goal (1) has the ball, and the play has shifted across the field. Defender (1) plays his man loosely, but moves in toward the crease. The goalie moves over to play the ball. The defenders in the danger zone press their men. Defenseman (3) realizes that he has moved too close to his man, but it is too late.

The attackman (3) breaks away from his defender and cuts for the crease, calling for a pass. The attacker behind the goal (1) sees his man in the clear and he passes. Defender (3) knows that he is beaten. He tries to pursue, but has to shout for help. The pass is caught at "X," but the defenders at the crease are already reacting to the call for help.

The attacker (3) has the ball and is running for the outside corner of the crease to make a shot. The defensive creaseman (2) drives forward and throws a hard bodycheck on the ball carrier (3). Defender (6) has moved up to the front of the crease to block the possible shot, and his teammate (4) has also moved in. The attacker (3), realizing that he has been foiled, manages to keep the ball, but is forced to run out from the crease.

his man and the goal *and* between his man and the ball. There is the possibility of the pass, and every defenseman knows it. If it is successful, it could be damaging.

Here is where talking is an important part of the defensive strategy. The defender on the man making the cut is confident that he has his man and is in total control of the pass and cut situation. But he must let the other defenders know this. He shouts, "I've got him!" In this way, the other defenders will stay with their own men.

With a pass imminent, the goalie is turned, facing the

man with the ball behind the goal. He is ready to shout
"Check!" if the pass is made. The other defense players are
ready to check their opponent's sticks.

The attack player behind the goal realizes that he cannot
make the pass safely, so he passes the ball to the second man
on the far side of the field behind the goal. Now the play
moves to that side of the field and the defense shifts.

The goalie shifts over to the opposite side of the net to
play the ball. The defender on the crease waiting to pick up
the man behind the goal now takes a step closer. He doesn't
go up on his man, but he is totally alert. The man with the ball
must run or pass. If he runs he is going to have to try a dodge,
or he might go around behind the goal. In either case, the
defender must be ready to either stop him or go with him.

Meanwhile, the mid-fielder who had first cut in the hope
of getting a pass has moved to the first attack position, and the
man at first attack shifted to the right side. Their defenders
are on them, but loosely, playing a stick-length back, ready
to help out if they are needed at the crease. The defender playing the mid-fielder on the left moves in to play his man closer.
He has placed himself between his man and the man behind
the goal to cut off a pass. But he has come too close, the middie
on the attack is fast, and there is a sudden cut.

The defensive player knows that he has been beaten. He
lunges after his man, but he is too late. The pass comes from
the man behind the goal and the middie takes it on the run.
Someone else is going to have to stop the shot on the goal.

Again, talking aids the defense. "A shooter, a shooter!"
the beaten defender shouts. It is all happening very fast, but
since all the defensive players are watching the man with the
ball, they see the cut, the pass, and the catch. The sideline defender is shouting that the man is loose and is going for the
shot.

The man on the crease steps out from his position to meet
the shooter. The defender guarding the man on the point drops

his man, who is out of the play at the moment, and rushes up to check the shot.

At the moment it is important to stop the shot on the goal. The creaseman puts a bodycheck on the shooter. The man is thrown off-stride. There is also another defender suddenly in position. The attacker veers off and runs out to the right. There is no shot. The defender beaten by the fast cut picks up his man.

Something the defensemen must be very careful about at this moment is the lull that comes after a successful defense of the goal, and the feeling that the attackmen must now regroup and mount another attack. A smart, aggressive attacking unit will take advantage of this momentary feeling of respite. In the play just described, the play has shifted to the right side of the field, with the defeated shooter running toward the centerline. It would be a perfect time for the man playing first attack position to break down the left side, which is open, call for a pass, and take a long shot on the left side of the goal. The defensemen must be ready for this; they must retrench very quickly and be set for the next attack.

Be Careful of Switching

There are times when defenders have to switch coverage from one man to another to stop a shot at the goal, but it is always a loaded move that can result in disaster. In the case just described, the shooter had beaten his man and was running for the uncovered goal. When the point defender dropped his man and picked up the shooter, there was another man who was not covered.

If the shooter had noticed this at the same time he knew he was not going to get a clean shot, he might have passed to the man on point who could possibly rush the crease and make a quick toss into the goal before his defender could react.

When a defender runs up against a screen, he will often shout "Switch!" to change men with the defender covering the screen. It can be a useful move for the defense unit, especially if the players are experienced and have played together for a long time. For new players, however, switching defense assignments can lead to total confusion with nobody covering his man because he isn't sure who he is supposed to be covering. It is a move that should be used sparingly, if at all.

Short-handed Defense

There comes a time for every defensive unit when one of their players is sidelined for an infraction of the rules and they have to defend the goal a man short. This calls for a stylized formation.

With one man out of the game, the defense forms a four-man box around the front of the crease, and the fifth man goes after the man with the ball, putting him under intense pressure. The object is to tie the attackman up so that he has to pass the bull. When he does this, the defender falls back to take up a position in the box at the crease, and the defender closest to the man who received the pass takes over the harassment duties.

If there are two men out of the game at the same time, the defense will be sorely pressed. It doesn't happen too often, but when it does alert attackers will swarm at the goal. In this case, the defensemen have only one recourse. They have to form a four-man box around the front of the crease and, with the goalie, meet the attack as it comes. They have to do their best to defend against it, hopefully picking off a shot as it comes in.

This formation forces the attackmen to shoot from the outside, increasing their chances of missing the goal.

CLEARING THE BALL

When the defensemen get the ball, they have to get it out of their goal area and into the other team's goal area as quickly as possible. This, as mentioned before, is called clearing.

In most cases, it is the goalkeeper who clears the ball. He can run the ball out toward the centerline, looking for an open man to pass to. He can pass directly from the crease. He can also run behind the goal, pass to a man on either side of the field, and then back him up if the attack unit decides to set up a ride. In every game you will see the goalie do all three. He adapts the clear to the situation that presents itself.

An important factor in a clear is for close defense players to assist the goalie. When the attackmen are putting pressure on the goalie, the defensive teammates must come back to him, moving in and around to make it easy for him to make the pass.

In a game played by experienced players, the long pass is often used to clear the ball. The theory is that the ball travels faster than any player can run, so if you want to mount a sudden attack out of a fast break, the long pass from the opposite end of the field is the way to do it. In a game played by beginners, the long pass is usually a good way to throw the ball away. Use it sparingly and only when you have picked out a receiver and know that you can reach him.

The short pass is the safest way to clear the ball, and combined with the run and dodge is an effective way to combat a close ride. The mid-fielders must get over the centerline and on the attack, but unless they already have the ball, they should pause at the centerline until the ball is cleared. The attack unit might be suddenly putting on a six-man ride, hoping to use two-on-one tactics to get the ball away from the defensemen before it can be cleared. In this case, the middies will be needed, and they should be close enough to quickly lend a hand.

Talking is very important in the clearing maneuver, with the goalie calling signals, shouting for help if he gets under too much pressure from a ride, and offering assistance if a defender is tied up after taking a pass.

Where a defensive unit has practiced the kind of teamwork that allows it to form, bend, and reform to fit a wide variety of attack situations, they are usually able to clear without difficulty.

A bad thing that can happen to a defensive unit is for the players to try to single out the culprit responsible for a missed ball or a shot at the goal, and to express their frustration with criticism. When players start blaming one another, you know that the defense is coming apart. If the team has a defensive captain, he should stop this sort of thing the moment it starts. It happens all too often with beginning players.

9

KEEPER OF THE GOAL

WHEN A team is on the defense, the goalie is like a music conductor. From his vantage point, he has a view of everything that is happening. He does not have to contend with an attack player, so his total attention is on the ball.

A good goalie is a good talker. He calls out every move that the attackers are making. He sees if a teammate is allowing himself to be fooled by a clever attack player, and he shouts a warning. If an artful dodger gets past his man, the goalie sings out, "A shooter!" to alert the defenders on the crease that an undefended attacker is coming in for a shot. When a pass has been made and the ball is in the air, the goalie shouts, "Check!" alerting the defensemen to check sticks. If he sees where the pass is going, he will call out the name of his teammate defending the receiver, telling him to check his man's stick.

Except for a chest pad, the goalie wears no special protective equipment. It takes a certain amount of courage to stand in the goal with a lacrosse ball being fired at you with great force, particularly when you are expected to use "any part of the body" to deflect the ball.

One advantage that the goalie has while he is inside the crease area is that no offensive player is allowed to step into the crease. Also, no player is allowed to make any contact with the goalkeeper or his crosse while he and the ball are within the crease area, whether he has the ball in his possession or not.

In addition to the regular protective gear, the goalie wears a chest protector. The face of his crosse is also considerably larger, giving him a slight advantage.

If the goalie steps out of the crease area, however, he can be treated like any other defensive player.

Every goalie has his own style of play, but there are some standard procedures that most effective goalies follow. He plays the ball at all times. When the ball is on one side of the field or the other, the goalie plays that side of the goal, usually out in front of the vertical standard.

The goalie's stick usually has a short handle, which allows him to shift the stick quickly. It also has a large face to help him in catching shots. With both hands on the stick and the face held vertical, the goalie tries to place himself directly in the path of any shot on the goal. If he catches the ball, he lets the crosse give a little, then gives it a quick twist. For ground balls, he must try to stop them with his feet or legs with the crosse suddenly swung down.

Most important, when the ball is brought into the crease area for an attempted shot, the goalie must have his eye on the ball every second. He must anticipate the shot. Will it be high to the right or left corner, a bouncer, a ground ball sneaking past a confusion of feet? When the shot comes, he must be there to meet it.

Alone in the crease, the goalie has only his own quick reactions to stop a shot like this. The ball can be seen going past his left shoulder, on the way to a score.

The goalie is in a good position for intercepting passes to and from the man on the point. When the ball is behind the net, he always turns to face the ball and he keeps his crosse high.

After a missed shot at the goal, the goalie should always be ready to go after a loose ball near the front of the crease. He has to make a quick judgment about his chances of getting the ball. He should not leave the crease to battle another player for possession of a loose ball, under any circumstances.

The goalie is the most important player in clearing the ball downfield. He is the extra man. If an attacker comes in to play him closely, he has to let a defensive player go uncovered.

Speed and agility are important characteristics of the lacrosse goalie. In clearing the ball he will often have to run the ball down to the centerline, zig-zagging, cutting, and dodging until he finds a receiver open to take the ball.

10

GIRLS' LACROSSE

T HERE IS a widespread feeling, particularly among players, that girls' lacrosse is totally different from boys' lacrosse. There is some truth to this belief regarding the rules of play and the way in which the game is conducted. In terms of basic skills, however, the two games are almost identical.

There is no contact allowed in the girls' game and no bodychecks or checking of sticks unless the player has possession of the ball. The girls wear no protective gear, except for the goalie, and their only equipment is the stick and usually a pair of soccer cleats. Girls still use the traditional handmade wooden stick, although some players are using a stick with the traditional shape, but with a plastic wall for more strength.

The old-style crosse has a very shallow pocket. The rules of the girls' game state that not more than one-half of the ball

Cradling the ball in the old-style crosse is more difficult. The girls run with the crosse in front of them, the pocket and the ball facing them.

can show below the wall, and the official checks each crosse before a game. It is more difficult to hold and carry the ball in the wooden stick, so in some ways it might be said that the girls' game requires greater skills. It takes longer to learn to throw with the wooden stick. There are also right- and left-handed sticks, so most girls play on their natural side.

Cradling is more difficult with the wooden stick, and this affects the style of play. It is rare that you will ever see a girl cradle the ball one-handed, as you see in the boys' game, and it is definitely frowned upon by all coaches.

But just as in the boys' game, if a girl can cradle and run with the ball, pass and catch effectively, scoop up loose balls, and cut and dodge, she can play on anybody's team.

The girls' game is closer to the original Indian game,

with the violence removed. There are no boundaries to the playing field, except what is decided upon before the game; there are a minimum of rules to break; and the girls are expected to play like ladies.

Because lacrosse has been played by women for as long as field hockey and goes back to the turn of the century, there is a natural reluctance to change the game to resemble the boys' game. Like field hockey, it is a game that places more emphasis on skill and speed and ball-handling abilities than on brute force. It is an exciting game to watch, particularly in today's social climate, where the girls can display aggressive athletic prowess, stamina, and speed, and not be critically stereotyped by antiquated attitudes.

As in boys' lacrosse, the objective of the game is to carry or pass the ball down the field with the crosse and deposit it in the goal at the other end, while a team of players are trying to get the ball away to do the same thing at the opposite end of the field.

Although there are no real boundaries in the girls' game, the goals (exactly like the boys') are usually 100 yards apart. There is a centerline between the two goals. Before the game the coaches and officials decide on the boundaries, but it is usually loosely defined and the official simply decides when a ball is out of bounds and stops play to have it thrown in. If a player has control of the ball, however, the officials seem to let her run wherever she feels like running, as long as she is eluding a player and trying to get to the goal. This makes for some spectacular runs.

There are twelve girls on a team. There are three defense players, besides the goalie, called *point, cover point*, and *third man*. There are five mid-fielders called *right defense wing, left defense wing, right attack wing, left attack wing*, and *center*. There are three attack players called *third home, second home*, and *first home*. With the exception of the goalie, these players have no restrictions on where they can play on the field, and

In girls' lacrosse, they use the standing face-off.

there are no rules about keeping a certain number of defense or attack players in their respective areas. In other words, there are no off-side penalties.

The game is started with a standing face-off at center field (draw). Both centers face on opposite sides of the centerline, their crosses meeting back-to-back about shoulder height. In some cases a girl will stand straddling the centerline, or both girls will be on the same side of the centerline. The important thing is that the faces of the two crosses be poised directly over the centermark on the field. The centers can take whatever pose they feel gives them the most power on the draw. The crosses, however, must be parallel with the centerline. The rule book only says: "The opponents each stand with one foot toeing the center line. The foot should be perpendicular to the line." The wooden walls of the crosses are touching at the bottom; the official drops the ball in between the two. All the other players, meanwhile, must be outside the center circle. In practice, the players form a circle around the two centers, each covered by an opposition player, each hoping to get the ball. They are motionless until play begins.

The official drops the ball and calls, "Draw!" and the two centers lift their crosses abruptly, trying to direct the ball to a teammate. The ball must go over their heads or the draw is replayed.

If the ball lands on the ground, the nearest players make a dash for it and try to scoop it up into their crosses. There can be no checking of a crosse until a player has the ball, but a careful player will pursue her opponent from behind, let her lift the ball, and then check, bringing her crosse down sharply over the throat of her opponent's stick, hopefully dislodging the ball. She'll then scoop it up with her own crosse.

We should point out here that in the girls' game checking a player's stick is also called *tackling*, an older expression. The two terms are interchangeable, but checking is now the more common word.

ATTACKING WITH THE BALL

When a player has possession of the ball, she runs with the crosse upright in front of her. One hand is at the bottom of the handle, the other is several inches below the throat. The crosse is tilted forward slightly to keep the ball in the pocket. The face of the crosse is toward the runner. She cradles the ball as she runs in the same manner that her male counterpart does.

Most girls' teams, especially on the secondary school level, use a minimum of strategy in their attack. They will usually keep two attack players down near the opposition goal, playing out on either side of the goal circle (it is not called a crease in the girls' game). When the attackers come down the field, two players will move to the goal circle, two more will take up positions far out from the sides of the goal, and the others will run around waving for the ball.

When the player with the ball runs for the goal, another player must try to defend against her without causing any physical contact. This isn't easy to do, and most officials are aware that there is bound to be some bodily contact. They overlook it as long as the contact is not intentional and is slight. The defensive player cannot block out the ball carrier, but, on the other hand, the ball carrier cannot charge a defender.

The defender should play the ball, keep the face of her crosse in the air, and check the attacker's crosse in an attempt to dislodge the ball and be ready to knock down an attempted pass. The attacker, on the other hand, must protect the ball, and if she can execute the roll dodge, it is usually very effective in the girls' game. She rolls off her defender, goes into the center, and takes a shot.

If the shot misses and there is a scramble for the loose ball, there will invariably be a whistle to stop the play. There can be no kicked balls, and there can be no hitting the ball along the ground. A scramble usually results in an impasse. The players must all freeze in position at the sound of the whistle, and they must not move from that position until play is resumed. If there happens to be an injury that looks like it will delay the game, the players put their sticks on the ground to mark their position so they can take the same place when play resumes. The official will take two players about five yards from the other players and at least 8.8 yards (8 meters) from the goal circle and place them with their crosses at least one yard apart. She stands off about five yards, and on the word, "Play!" she tosses the ball to the two players who try to get possession of it. This is called a *throw*.

If there is a foul on a play, the player fouled is given a *free position*. This is an opportunity for the player to take the ball into play with no opposition from the other team. When the whistle blows signaling a foul, all play stops and the players freeze in position. The official indicates where the player taking the free position is to stand and where the offending player is to stand. The offender is placed about five yards from the player taking the free position, in the direction from which she approached before committing the foul. No player may be closer than 4.4 yards to the player taking the free position. All players must be moved away. No free position can be taken closer than 8.8 yards to the goal circle. If the foul occurs in what is known as the Critical Scoring Area, which is a loosely defined area around the goal and twenty yards in front of the goal, then a lane is cleared between the player given the free position and the goal (penalty lane). The official gives the offended player the ball. She places it in her crosse. The official says, "Play!" and the game is resumed. If the player is close to the goal, she may take a shot, realizing, of course, that opposing players will extend their crosses into the penalty lane the second that play is resumed. She may also run or pass the ball.

When the defenders of the goal get the ball, the roles are reversed, and they pass or run the ball down the field to attack the opposition goal. This is exactly the same as in the boys' game.

The length of the girls' game is usually fifty minutes, but this can be reduced to forty minutes if the coaches and officials agree before the game. The game is played in two halves (no quarters), and there is a ten-minute break between the halves. There are not supposed to be any substitutions except at the half, but this rule can be waived if coaches and officials agree on open substitutions at the beginning of the game. Once a player comes out of the game, however, she cannot go back in until after the half-time break.

DEFENDING AGAINST ATTACK

There is a rule in girls' lacrosse that adds to the difficulty of defending the goal. This is the existence of the *shooting lanes*. A shooting lane is a path to the goal as defined by two lines extending from the ball to the two goalposts. This is supposed to be kept open, and if a defender places herself in the path of the ball traveling to the goal, she can be called for a foul.

The attacker should be tied up and checked long before she gets into position to shoot. Once she is in the shooting lane, the defenders can only reach out to block the shot with their sticks, or the defense is in the hands of the goalie.

Keeping the shooting lanes clear, on the other hand, benefits the goalie, who has a clear view of the shot. A good goalie never takes her eye off the ball until it has gone to the opposite end of the field. She is the last position of defense and she must make a lot of catches and deflections. Her protective equipment consists of helmet, mask, and full padding down to her

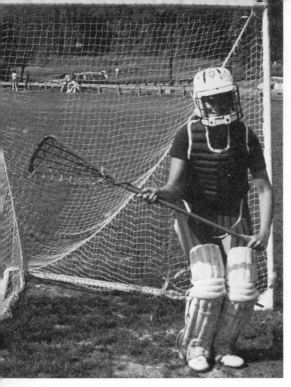

The goalie in girls' lacrosse is the only player wearing protective equipment. Although she must try to stop goals with a normal-sized crosse, she wears a helmet and face guard, and complete body and leg padding.

shoes, but she carries only the regular size wooden crosse, unlike her male counterpart, whose crosse looks like a basket.

No player except the goalie is allowed in the goal circle, and she is not allowed to be touched while she is in the circle. It is also a rule that shots at the goal cannot be fired with "dangerous speed." Even so, when the defense unit has allowed the attackers to get close enough to shoot, it is a tough day for the goalie.

TRAIN LIKE THE BOYS

It should be apparent to anyone examining the girls' game of lacrosse that their play will benefit from the exercises, techniques, and simple strategies practiced by the boys' teams.

There should be endless drills on passing and catching. The girls should line up facing in two lines. As a girl comes running, a facing player throws a pass. The girl catches it and throws it back. This is repeated until the players can snap up the ball and have it cradled in the same movement.

Scooping the ball is as important for the girls as it is for the boys. You must learn to run in a crouch so you can get your stick down and scoop the ball on the run, getting under it and using follow-through, and keeping the end of the handle down. A good exercise for this is to stand in a line and hold the crosses at arm's length out to the side and touching the ground. The player at the front turns and runs the length of the line, having to stoop under the outstretched arms of her teammates.

The girls practice in pairs going after the loose ball. One girl goes out ahead and a second girl follows a couple of seconds later. The first girl scoops the ball and the second girl must check her stick.

As in the boys' game, passing and catching while on the run are a constant at all practice sessions or game warm-ups.

An exercise that teaches the players to run low with their heads down to scoop a ball; the players run under the outstretched arms at top speed.

Going after the loose ball, one player goes for the ball and her opponent closes in to check her stick.

After taking a pass, the offensive player tries to outrun the impending check from the defender. The defender's stick must not touch the player.

Defending against passes is something that can be practiced by the hour. This is tough in the girls' game because the defender cannot make a move to check until the attacker has the ball. The defense must be an interception or a check of the stick just after the catch.

Passing the ball back and forth is as much a basic practice for the girls' game as for the boys'. In the girls' game, they also use the underhand shovel pass seen here.

Passing the ball back and forth between players is important in the girls' game too, and the hours of playing catch with a teammate will always pay off. Finding a wall to practice against is a great way to sharpen ball-handling skills.

Cut and pass plays are valuable in both games, but you don't see them executed consistently in the girls' game. A wise coach should study the boys' game, especially in the cut and dodge plays, and then work her girls until they are experts at the moves. The object of lacrosse, whether boys' or girls', is for the players to break clear of their defenders and assault the goal. There is no more effective way to do it than the cut and dodge when it is properly done.

Practicing to cut, the player with the ball is making a sharp turn to the right. The approaching defender is moving fast and will easily be passed.

The roll dodge is just as effective for the girls as for the boys. Here the player takes a pass over her shoulder with a defender close between her and the crease. As she cradles the ball, she pivots and rolls to the inside, beating her opponent and moving into scoring territory.

Everything in this book, with the exception of the body contact play, can be quickly modified to fit the rules of the girls' game and will make any team a more effective unit on attack or defense.

Glossary

BODYCHECK	Hitting an opponent with your shoulder.
BUTT	The end of the handle of the crosse.
CENTER	A circled area at centerfield where the face-off is held to start the game and to resume play after quarters and half-time.
CENTER LINE	A line dividing the field into two equal parts.
CHECKING	Deflecting an opponent's stick with your own.
CLEARING	Getting the ball out of the defensive side of the field and into the hands of the attack unit.
CLOSE ATTACK	The three players who lead the offensive against an opponent's goal.
CLOSE DEFENSE	The three players whose primary duty is to protect their goal.

CRADLING	Twisting movement of the crosse used to hold the ball in the pocket.
CREASE	A circle around the goal where only the goal tender and defensive players may tread.
CROSSE	The stick used in the game of lacrosse.
CROSSE CHECK	Illegally pushing an opponent with the handle of the crosse.
CUTTING	A maneuver in which a player eludes his defender by running in one direction and then suddenly changing direction with a sharp turn.
DODGING	Maneuver in which a player eludes his defender by making a movement in one direction and then turning or running in the opposite direction.
FACE	The wide part of the crosse where the ball is handled.
FACE-OFF	When two players of opposing teams are brought together to struggle for possession of the ball.
FORCING	An aggressive movement by a defensive player to make an attack player pass or run before he is ready.
GOAL AREA	An area that extends twenty feet from each end of the field and ten yards in from the sidelines.
HEAD	The flat leading edge of the crosse face.
MIDFIELD	The three players who assist on both the attack and defense.
OFF-SIDE	When one team has more than six players on one side of the field at the same time.
PASS	Using the crosse to throw the ball to another player.
POCKET	The portion of the net on the crosse where the ball is carried.

POINT	Defensive position behind and to either side of the goal.
RECEIVING	Catching a pass with the crosse.
RIDING	Playing a defensive unit closely and aggressively to keep them from clearing the ball.
SCOOPING	Lifting the ball off the ground with the crosse.
SCREEN	Using a teammate as a shield against a defensive player when making a pass.
SHOOTING	Throwing the ball at the goal.
SLASHING	Illegally striking an opponent with the crosse.
SLIDING	When a defensive player leaves the man he is guarding to defend against a player closer to the goal.
THROAT	The part of the crosse where the face joins the handle.
WALL	The sides of the face on the crosse.
WING	The area near the sidelines and center-line where midfield players are stationed during a face-off at center.

Index

ABOUT THE AUTHOR

STUART JAMES has been writing for twenty-five years. Although he has been principally a magazine journalist, he has also authored ten novels and five books of nonfiction. He lives in Greenwich, Connecticut, and now writes exclusively for young readers.